The Origins of
Lexham Gardens
and
Lee Abbey in London

The Origins of Lexham Gardens and Lee Abbey in London

David Weekes

Gracewing.

Any profits from the sale of this book will go towards the renovation of the Chapel at Lee Abbey in London.

The writer will be most grateful for any information or illustrations which might be relevant to a revised edition of this book.

First published in 1996

Gracewing
Fowler Wright Books
2 Southern Avenue, Leominster
Herefordshire HR6 0QF

ISBN 0 85244 361 7

Typeset by Action Typesetting Limited, Gloucester
Printed by Cromwell Press, Broughton Gifford, Wiltshire

Contents

Preface

During 1995–96 the Lee Abbey Movement marks its
Golden Jubilee. In 1945 the Lee Abbey estate on the coast
of North Devon was purchased, and the first guests were
welcomed there in 1946. Many connected with the movement in various ways will gather in London on the 8th
June 1996 to celebrate.

By that date Lee Abbey will also have been active in
Kensington, working among students from all parts of the
world for thirty two years. It is more than time that there
was a separate publication about this aspect of the Lee
Abbey vision.

Then in April 1995 Lexham Gardens and the immediate
vicinity, became a conservation area. This realised the
hopes of many residents that something more would be
done to ensure the preservation of Lexham Gardens and
frustrate any further attempts at insensitive redevelopment.

Local inhabitants, as well as many of those who stay here
at Lee Abbey, will be curious about this small area of
Kensington, and they will find it hard to discover any
readily available account of Lexham Gardens, or of Lee
Abbey which since 1982 has housed its London operations
at the interconnected houses which are numbered 57–67.

This short account has been put together to satisfy this
commendable curiosity. It has been written during my
own first year here, and there will be shortcomings from so
brief a residence. Despite that limitation it seems better to

make it available now, and to amend it later if need be, rather than to delay. My wife has shared in the adventure of coming to live in Kensington and with love and gratitude I dedicate this little book to her.

August 1995
DW

Nos. 57–75 Lexham Gardens typical elevation: Samuel J. Wyand, builder, 1875 (measured and drawn by Roy Bowles and Michael F. Clements)

1

The Background

By Way of Introduction

This is the story of one hundred and twenty five tall mid-Victorian houses, the road in which they stand, and how they all came into being in what we would now call a 'green field site'. It tells how these family homes, in a fashionable part of London, came to be inhabited; what kind of people lived here, and how later on, six separate dwellings came to be transformed into one house to provide a home for students from all over the world.

This book falls into two sections which overlap at times. If you are particularly interested in Lexham Gardens, read the first part. If it is Lee Abbey that you are more curious about, you will find out much by reading the second part. Behind both lies the Christian faith, and the beliefs which that faith inspires in people past and present. Those who first built here stood firmly in that tradition. The evidence for this is all around us in this part of London. The ancient parish of St Mary Abbots stretched over a wide rural area. During the developments of the Nineteenth Century this was divided into no fewer than fourteen parishes each with its own church, and many of the great housing developments are still dominated by a large central church, like those just south of Cromwell Road: St Jude's, Courtfield Gardens; St Mary, The Boltons; and St Luke's, Redcliffe Square. In our area there was no need for a church in

Lexham Gardens since at the west end there was St Philip's, just around the corner in Earl's Court Road, and a little to east, Christ Church in Victoria Road, which still belonged to St Mary Abbots. Both had been built in the 1850s and St Philip's very soon had to be enlarged from its one thousand seats to fourteen hundred, with several services each Sunday, all of them packed with people. Lexham Gardens is now split in two at Marloes Road by these parish boundaries. Still today, those who run Lee Abbey here are 'not ashamed of the gospel of Christ' as St Paul tells us that we should not be.

At the same time we seek to provide a home for students of all faiths, or of none. The same mixture of human attitudes will be found all around us now in this part of London, which is so cosmopolitan. So many people come to stay here for a few months, or a few years, as they study at their courses, and prepare for their careers in the future. Others pass through on holiday for only a night or two. All humanity is here, and this little book attempts to clothe the background of this place with a little human interest too. If we believe that God is the Creator, every human being is of equal worth in his sight. Whatever our own beliefs, this should be a house in which we can live together in peace and tolerance, seeking to understand each other, perhaps learning from one another, but respecting each other too. Anything we can do to understand each other better will further this atmosphere in which racial and national barriers are broken down. It is in this spirit that this little book has been put together.

The Wider Location

This is written for those of you who are curious to know something about the part of London in which you are staying. We are conveniently situated very close to some of the outstanding features in this capital city, and you are only a few minutes walk away from Kensington Gardens, one of the Royal parks, which leads on eastwards into Hyde Park and so into central London. Indeed you can walk on to Trafalgar Square and Westminster Abbey, almost entirely through royal parks in little more than an hour. The distance is only three and a half miles. Hardly further away than Kensington Palace (set in the Gardens) is the Royal Albert Hall, an enormous concert hall famous above all for the Promenade Concerts held there every year from July to September. Just to the south you will find the Science and Natural History Museums, and the Victoria and Albert Museum of fine arts and crafts beside them. A little to the west of us are Earl's Court Stadium and Olympia. All around are dignified streets of tall houses like these in Lexham Gardens. Today this forms part of the Abingdon Ward of the Royal Borough.

One Thousand Years Ago

However if we look back over the last one thousand years of history, Kensington has only recently become a part of the city. In 1000. A.D. London had been an important port and centre since Roman times under the Emperor Claudius, and had by now become of such consequence for kings to be acclaimed and crowned here. With the Norman Conquest of 1066 the first detailed record of England was made through the *Domesday Book* (1086). Though only eight miles from the Tower of London which the Conqueror built, Kensington remained an entirely rural and largely undeveloped area. In *Domesday* it is 'Chenesitun', probably from a Saxon community or person called 'Chenesi'. The survey gives us other interesting details. Before the Conquest the land was held by Edwin, a thane of King Edward 'the Confessor'. With William the Conqueror, Kensington ceased to be royal land; he gave it to the church in the person of Geoffrey,

Bishop of Coutances, one of his cities in Normandy.
Together with Lanfranc of Canterbury, Geoffrey was one
of the King's most trusted governors of both church and
state affairs. Aubrey de Vere, ancestor of the legendary
family of the Earls of Oxford which finally died out in
1703, held it from the Bishop. Ver is a village ten miles
south of Coutances. Within a few years Aubrey came to
hold the estate in his own right. He seems to have been
married to a half-sister of the Conqueror. He in turn gave
a central part of the estate to the Abbey of Abingdon in
Oxfordshire. For this reason the parish was renamed St
Mary Abbots. This family never lived here, but their Court
came to be held in the manor house from which it took its
name. There were few buildings, apart from a little cluster
near where Earl's Court Station now stands. The culti-
vated land was only sufficient for ten ploughs. Apart from
the manor there were only eighteen villagers, six with
three virgates of land and twelve with one, each being
about 30 acres, and there would be their families. One
priest and seven slaves are also recorded, and in the whole
area perhaps no more than two hundred people. There was
meadow, and 'pasture for the village livestock', plenty of
woodland (no doubt still natural forest) and 200 pigs.
There was no mill, but an interesting detail is 'three arpents
of vines' (about three acres). The total value of the land is
given as ten pounds!

Kensington has really gone through three periods.
Before and after the Norman Conquest in 1066 it was a
stretch of countryside, with fields and woods, entirely rural
in character, the Manor House, and the farm with its own
separate group of buildings. Much of this remained until
the time when Lexham Gardens was being made. Most of
the old buildings were demolished before 1880 to allow for
new ones to be put up.

Crest of the Vere family

Two Crucial Royal Influences on Kensington

The second period overlaps with the first to some extent. At the end of the Middle Ages some of the great English families built large houses in this quiet rural area as country retreats outside of the city. It was in this context that the Royal period began. Indeed Royal influence became so strong in the area that when Leigh Hunt published a book about Kensington in 1851 he called it *The Old Court Suburb*. Kensington began to be really well known after William of Orange became King of Great Britain in 1689, as William III, through his wife Queen Mary a daughter of James II. To get away from Whitehall he bought Nottingham House, one of the country houses which already existed, and he developed this into Kensington Palace. Courtiers needed houses nearby and so the little hamlets which had developed on the old de Vere lands began to grow, and the village of Kensington expanded with its church, its High Street and its Square. Thus it became the suburb of the court of the King. However the greatest changes came about during the Nineteenth Century. This area of large country houses, and market gardens serving London, became a focus of the activity of the husband and Consort of Queen Victoria, who had been born in Kensington Palace. Prince Albert was the moving force behind the Great Exhibition of 1851 held in Hyde Park. An amazing glass pavilion called the Crystal

Palace was built especially to house it there. So these two factors are unique in Kensington's development. If there had not been a royal palace, with the vast expanse of royal parks, the Great Exhibition would not have been held in Hyde Park, and its great profits would not have financed other projects in the locality. From this initiative developed others like the founding of the great museums, the Royal Colleges of Music and Art, and the Imperial College of Science and Technology. The Royal Albert Hall was later to be built in his memory.

The Railways and Residential Kensington

Earlier in the Nineteenth Century the third great period had begun in which almost all of the remaining fields were built upon, largely with residential houses. Some of the land-owning families who had succeeded the de Veres saw their chance to cash in on a building boom. One of these was the Edwardes family, who had inherited the estate centred on Holland House, set in what remains of Holland Park at the top of Earl's Court Road. Later the house and nearby lands were sold to the Fox family whose head became Lord Holland. Thus the Holland Park estate was divided into two. The head of the Edwardes family became Lord Kensington, and he retained lands a little to the south of Holland Park. Fairly early in the Century his son, the second Lord Kensington, began to allow builders to develop housing areas on parts of this estate. Later on a major impetus was given to further development. The early underground railways served this area well, and provided excellent communications for those who came to live here. In particular the Metropolitan District Railway was built between 1865–69, with a station at Earl's Court. Curiously enough, the railways were a mixed blessing for the new houses built in Kensington. Unless there were strong reasons for living really close to Central London, prosperous families often preferred to move out into suburbs, or countryside, where conditions were cleaner, land more plentiful, and freehold easier to obtain.

The Rural Estate Becomes an Urban Development

The first development of any part of the Edwardes estate for residential housing purposes came well before the railways. It was called Edwardes Square. The second Lord Kensington appointed an emigre Frenchman, Louis Leon Changeur, to be his agent for this purpose and an agreement was entered into in 1811. This was while the Napoleonic Wars were still raging, and Changeur was quickly confused with an infamous Colonel Charmilly. This mistake was soon sorted out, but it gave rise to the a story that the Edwardes Square houses were being built at the time of the threatened French invasion for the purpose of housing junior officers of Napoleon's army once it had been successfully carried out. Leigh Hunt, who lived in the Square later on, gave currency to this story in his book about Kensington already mentioned, saying that 'it was allowable for French imaginations in those days to run a little wild, on the strength of Napoleon's victories.' Hunt was an American, and the story is an amusing fiction for Changeur's agreement came six years after the Battle of Trafalgar, in October 1805, which effectively ended any real French hopes of invading England.

Oddly enough, a few years before his father's death, Captain William Edwardes had earned the thanks of the Prince Regent for his part in frustrating the last invasion of Great Britain, a small French affair on the Welsh coast in 1797. Four years later he inherited as the second Lord Kensington, and lived out his life as a curious and ultimately tragic figure. He was the only child of his father who was about sixty five years older than his son; his relationship has been compared with that of King George III and his eldest son, the Prince Regent. Young Edwardes was already running up large debts before his father's death. He began by following him in politics as M.P. for Haverfordwest and was briefly a Lord of the Admiralty in 1806–07. He was convinced that his father had cheated him out of owning the vast mansion of Holland House (largely destroyed by bombs dropped during the Second World War). He was enormous in size, and equally extensive in his spending, running up large debts which were secured against his lands. He was known by the nick-name 'Og', after the king of Bashan who was the last of the giants (*Deuteronomy* 3.11). Only a settlement of 1833 which entailed his estates upon his son and future descendants preserved them from the poverty in which he died in a house on his own Kensington estate in 1852.

The Edwardes family coat-of-arms, adapted from Fielding's *Peerage* (1783)

The Baron Kensington (1776)

Arms – Quarterly: 1st and 4th, ermine, a lion rampant, sable; for Edwardes, 2nd and 3rd, gules, a chevron, between three crosses-bottony or. *Crest* – Upon a mount, vert, a wyvern argent. *Supporters* – Two reindeer proper, attired and unguled, or. *Motto* – Garde la foi.

2

The Beginnings of
Lexham Gardens

The Curious Shape

Edwardes Square developed very gradually, taking fully a decade to complete. Changeur went bankrupt and fled back to France in 1813. Only slowly was the remainder of the estate turned over from agriculture to building, mainly in the second half of the century and most intensely after the coming of the underground railway. Our part of the district was among the last to be put to new use. Most of the Edwardes' land lay on the west side of Earl's Court Road, but a long finger extended to the east and Lexham Gardens was built along this, which accounts for the rather curious shape of the street (see pages 10–11).

The development of the eastern finger of land on the estate could not be accomplished until Cromwell Road had been extended westwards from Gloucester Road to link up with what is now called West Cromwell Road, but which already existed in those days as Fenelon Road. This new extension was completed in 1869. In October of that year plans were submitted for the area north of this new road. Wright's Lane turning south out of Kensington High Street, was joined up with Cromwell Road, and this extension became Marloes Road. Crossing this was Lexham Road (as it was first called) which traversed the area from Earl's Court Road in the west, and finally curved

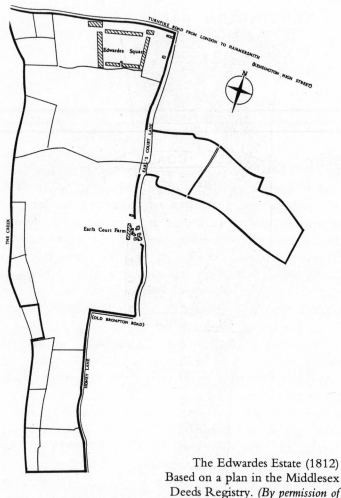

The Edwardes Estate (1812)
Based on a plan in the Middlesex
Deeds Registry. *(By permission of
the Royal Commission on the
Historical Monuments of England
RCHME))*

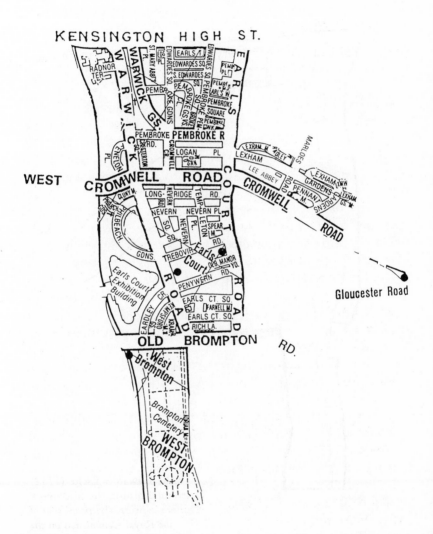

The same area today.

southwards to enter Cromwell Road in the east, the tip of the finger having been sold for railway development around Gloucester Road a few years earlier.

Why 'Lexham'?

In 1980 our local Library re-published *Kensington and Chelsea Street Names*. Out of around eight hundred street names altogether, the origins of some three hundred and fifty had by then been traced, though not always with real certainty. Lexham Gardens does not appear in the list given. Most of the names on the Edwardes Estate have connections with that family and their lands in Pembrokeshire, and the third Lord Kensington certainly took a personal hand in this. Earl's Court, from the feudal activity of the de Veres, and Old Manor Place both relate to the earlier history of the area, while St Mary Abbots Place was named after the Edwardes family ownership had ended. Holland Park had earlier been in the possession of a family called Rich, who were Earls of Warwick. Rich Lane and Warwick Road commemorate this family through whom the Holland Park and Earl's Court Estates came by marriage into the possession of those who gave their name to Edwardes Square.

Most of the remaining streets have names which come from Pembrokeshire. The third Lord Kensington's grandmother came from Longridge. Marloes is the village near to his country seat at St Brides on the Dale Peninsular, where he lived. Philbeach was one of his farms near there. Nevern, Penywern, Templeton, and Trebovir are also names from Pembrokeshire, lying far to the west of London. What then of Lexham? It is not known to have a Welsh background. It seems that one must rather look to the opposite point of the compass. East and West Lexham are villages in Norfolk, the county from which our principal builder, Wyand, had come, and some street names were provided by the builders. Logan Place, opposite the west end of Lexham Gardens, is probably one example, for William George Logan was 'a banker intimately connected with speculative building in South Kensington.' Indeed Wyand's fellow builder, John Sprake, applied for permission to lay out Lexham Mews in 1873, but the map accompanying shows another projected mews to the east which is labelled 'Wyand Mews'. In fact this eventually became Radley Mews, but it demonstrates the point.

It is tempting therefore to look for a connection with Wyand and Norfolk when it came to naming Lexham Road. He originated from Halvergate in Norfolk. Perhaps his mother's family came from the Lexhams? However all of this seems increasingly unlikely when we discover that the name Lexham Road had already been given by October 1869, at least a year before building plots were negotiated. Then why was this Norfolk name chosen? One possibility is that it is known that the second Lord Kensington had owned or rented Heydon Hall in Norfolk. He had disputed the sale of Holland Park, but in 1823 had finally given that up and was living at Heydon. His heir, the third baron, was nearing seventy when Lexham Road was named, and had been a young naval officer in those far off days. Heydon is twenty miles from the Lexhams, but perhaps there was a connection between these places through people, which was remembered forty years later.

The word Lexham itself is easy to explain. It means homestead (ham) of the leech or physician, from the Old English for leech, the blood-sucking worm (see page 33) formerly used by doctors, who were given that nick-name.

This Area of Kensington as a Development

When one of the most prominent builders of houses in South Kensington (Sir Charles Freake) died in 1884, it was said that he had raised the neighbourhood from 'a neglected suburb to the rank of a second Belgravia.' Lexham Gardens was built at the end of the great building boom in Kensington which seems to have peaked in 1875. Moreover the type of house built here, the large family home, also seems to have gone out of fashion about the same time. As early as 1878 it was professionally observed that there are 'at the present moment acres of large mansions at South Kensington empty, but finished. Two out of every three builders have failed or are on the verge of it.' Those who sought houses in this area were 'either those who valued the convenience, facility and reputation of Kensington or those who had to be close to their work. On the strength of the former, parts of South Kensington retained their standing for years to come.'

Speculative Building

Lexham Gardens was one of the last parts of the Edwardes Estate to be developed. Beginning in 1870 agreements were entered into which eventually led to eight different builders or building firms erecting houses during the years 1872–84. Though they vary in size, in facade the houses are all of the typical mid-Victorian Italianate design with four or five storeys above a basement, some with a small sixth storey which may be set back between the chimneys. Usually they are built with the portico and entrance on the left, but occasionally they are built in mirrored pairs, as at Nos. 82–84, and some of the houses on the south-eastern curve into Cromwell Road are also of this design (see Plates 2b, 4c and page 30).

Builders were in a precarious position. They had to raise the necessary finance to build and then be successful in finding buyers or tenants, so that there was return upon the money laid out, much of which had been borrowed. There was a leasehold system peculiar to London. The Landowner's agent, in our case M. J. Stutely acting for

Lord Kensington, would divide up the land and lease it to a number of builders. For the first few years, while the builder was developing the plot, the rent for leasing the land would be very low. Once the houses were ready the builder would sell them off to investors, or lease or sell them to private buyers. The builder would then have made his profit, and the landowner would receive a proper rent for the land. At the end of the lease, usually ninety-nine years, the landowner would get back the land and the houses built on it. Thus the land effectively remained in his family. He probably received a better rent than for agricultural land and in the end there was the profit of having a house to sell, usually again in leasehold, so that the process began all over again. It was the builder who took the risk. Towards the end of the 1870s there was a slump in the housing market in South Kensington, with the runaway bankruptcy in 1878 of Corbett and McClymont, one of the largest companies involved. Their liabilities were a staggering £1,300,000. Three of the builders in Lexham Gardens became bankrupt a few years after completing their houses here.

Further details of the builders will interest some more than others. Some, too, will want to know more of the design of the facades as we view them from the street, or of the lay-out of the interiors, and the way of life that these houses were intended to support (see Chapter Four, and the Appendix – page 91).

Why Gardens?

The plans for Lexham Road were altered in 1877 to include the communal garden which is such a feature of the east end before the road curves south (see 1879 map on page 18). No doubt there were good reasons for the revised layout. Those responsible may well have had the sense to realise that the housing market in South

Kensington was becoming over-stocked and that further measures were needed to ensure that the houses remaining to be built on the north side, eastwards from Marloes Road, would find occupiers, in an enterprise which was becoming increasingly competitive.

The better areas of housing in West London had been laid out in squares or in crescents. The 'gardens' were a later development. Increasingly the plots allocated were being built over with large houses, leaving little open ground. Lexham Gardens demonstrates this. No longer were there front gardens, but porticoes leading straight onto the street. Even the area of land at the back might be greatly reduced by the advantage of having an extensive ground floor over the basement (as in Nos. 57–75). In any case the back gardens were narrow and never very large. Such development could appear to be undesirable, since one of the attractions of South Kensington had been its rather leafy rural aspect, and this was being lost as building progressed. One way to ameliorate this was by a 'Gardens'. In this lay-out some of the houses faced onto a central area in which tall trees could grow and a more extensive area of greenery could be nurtured. This became a communal, but not a public, facility. It was accessible only to adjacent householders who were given a key in return for sharing in the upkeep. In this way something of the amenity of a square could be provided, without so much loss of land:

> In this system of unbuilt-up garden-squares the layout of London's residential quarter may almost be described as exemplary and what is lost in the way of long vistas down the streets is regained in this immense benefit to health. One glance at the map of London speaks volumes here, and especially when it is compared with the map of Berlin, shows up the short-sighted policy pursued in the German capital, where the few green squares that exist are still being sold off as building-land.
>
> (H. Muthesius)

There may also have been a concern to make the eastern end of the development more attractive in view of the disadvantage of having the pollution from steam engines in the vicinity. In his book, *Jam Tomorrow*, Sir Basil Bartlett (born 1905) looked back on childhood visits to our end of Cornwall Gardens, remembering that 'the trees and bushes were mainly black, as they were regularly covered with soot from the nearby Metropolitan Railway.' This stretch of the Underground was not powered by electricity until after the Twentieth Century had begun. The communal garden is open only to key holders who live in the houses which overlook it: Nos. 27–53 and 32–88, and No.1 Lexham Walk. The exclusion of No.55 seems a little hard!

The houses on the northerly stretch were begun only after the plan was changed to include the 'garden' in 1877, and on the 1st March 1878 the name of the whole street was changed from Lexham Road to Lexham Gardens. At the same time many houses were re-numbered, as this had got into a real muddle with the original number 1 at the Earl's Court Road end and the odd numbers also starting at the Cromwell Road end as they still do today (see pages 100–101).

The Design of Lexham Gardens

The writer does not find himself in agreement with the criticisms of Hermann Muthesius (see below page 42) or of the editors of the *Survey of London* who concluded that

> the Victorian element in the streets of Kensington so preponderates that the earlier and later areas – of smaller, simpler houses behind blossoming front gardens, or the more wayward and individual houses of twentieth century architects – seem to relieve what is felt as monotony. This is so even though the main period of Kensington's building, from the 1850s to the 1880s, produced a great variety of facade-treatments to beguile the passer by. Grey or brown brick, stone and stucco were used in varying

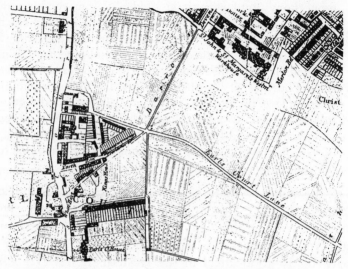

Extract from Daw's map of the parish of St Mary Abbots of 1867. It shows the fields between the workhouse to the north, and Earl's Court Lane (roughly the line of Cromwell Road), traversed by the lane called Barrows, which was soon to be replaced by Marloes Road.

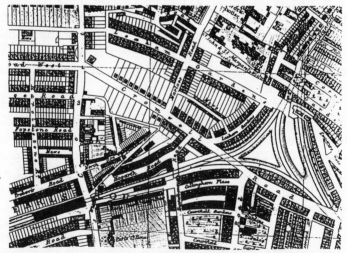

Extract from a similar map of 1879 showing Lexham Gardens, recently re-named from being originally called Lexham Road, and newly built over, apart from the northern stretch eastwards of Marloes Road.

proportions (until everything suddenly went red or red-yellow about 1882-83) ... But for all that the effect of much of Kensington is more wearisome than can be explained by a comparison of the facade designs. This results, perhaps, from the mere height of the houses acting in conjunction with the general busyness of a harsh and routine Italianate decoration. At street level the astonishing ubiquity of the pillared portico makes, in total, for tedium, particularly as the order chosen was usually a stolid Roman Doric that precluded the fluting of the columns which adds a welcome touch of sharpness to the equally plethoric Italianate of Bayswater.

On the contrary there is a satisfying comfort in the solid sentinels of these Doric columns guarding the doorways in such regular fashion, below the high walls of the multi-storeyed buildings on either side. This is shown to particularly good effect in the western stretch of Lexham Gardens between Marloes Road and Earl's Court Road.

Secondly, anyone who ambles through the area immediately north of that section of Lexham Gardens will see a great variety of housing all built in the period between about 1850 and 1880. Eastwards too there is Cornwall Gardens, and a little to the north some of the housing around Christ Church, also dates from as late as the 1850s. It cannot be said that there is any great monotony throughout this district though it is so Victorian.

Moreover, whenever the streets are relieved by trees as all good building should be, the effect can be entrancing, more especially when varieties bloom in Spring. Long ago, when it was still possible to stand on the rising ground of Kensington Gardens, and look down towards the Thames away to the south, Thomas Tickell wrote about it in the opening lines of a long poetic fantasy:

> Where Kensington high o'er the neighb'ring lands
> 'Midst greens and sweets, a Regal fabric stands,
> And sees each Spring, luxuriant in her bowers,
> A snow of blossoms, and a wilde of flowers.

Even today we still enjoy such wonders. In a neighbour-hood where once the hedgerows and the market gardens provided this natural bounty we can enhance the beauty by actively engaging in the schemes for planting more trees.

The Mews

Lexham Gardens is set about by small streets called Mews. The original concept of a mews was of an area behind the residential properties where stabling for carriages and horses was provided, over which the coachman, and per-haps other staff, could be accommodated. So we have Lexham Mews, Radley Mews, Pennant Mews, and Lexham Gardens Mews. Originally these were not open to through traffic. Sadly there are no remains of the iron containers for manure outside each of the stables.

Our houses were built in a period of transition. Some who could afford their own conveyance and staff needed stabling nearby. However, with such excellent facilities on the underground railways now easily available many trav-elled by train for daily needs. If they preferred to travel by road there were omnibuses, hansom cabs, or private carriages hired from a livery stables, all readily available, and all horse-drawn at this time. (See Plates 3c and 14b.)

Early Occupants

The first records from the Street *Directory* (1875) show only two houses in occupation. Almost certainly the first resi-dent was at number 1 (now No.146). Appropriately enough this was the first Vicar of St Philip's, Earl's Court Road, the Reverend J. D. Claxton. He had been Vicar for twenty years and died two years later at the early age of 48. The western part of Lexham Road (as it then was) had just become part of this parish, one of the many which had been formed within the original parish of St Mary Abbots

as the population expanded from the middle of the nineteenth century onwards. The *Directory* for 1876 lists four
other names. Three of these men, a barrister, a serving
Captain in the army, and a merchant remained here for
many years. They were very typical of the solid,
respectable middle, and upper middle class people who
came to live here. Only a few were minor members of the
aristocracy: in the 1881 Census we have Major the
Honourable Thomas O'Grady at No.12, 'son of a
Viscount' as he describes himself, and the Honourable
Hamilton Tollemache at No.144 a practising barrister.

Of lawyers there were plenty. Sidney Woolf was here
fairly early on at No.101 (1880–1892), being driven daily
by 'Dennis, the coachman' from 'the mews at the far end
near Cornwall Gardens ... Every morning immediately
after breakfast ... in his brougham from Lexham Gardens
to King's Bench Walk, where he had his chambers, and
every evening at six the brougham fetched him back just in
time for dinner ...' Daniel Fearon was long established at
No. 5 (re-numbered No. 142) from 1879–1900. He
became Secretary to The Charity Commission in 1885,
and later a Companion of the Order of the Bath. His
younger brother was Headmaster of Winchester.

Alexander Dauney, for many years at No.6 (1879–
1895?) was a bencher of the Middle Temple. Sir Henry
Sutton, at No.45 from 1879–1920, became a justice of the
High Court. Sir Henry Curtis Bennett, Chief Metropolitan
Magistrate lived at No.118 (1887–1913). His memorial, in
brass with raised lettering and an alabaster frame, is on the
inside South wall of St Philip's. He died very suddenly 'at
the Mansion House while in the midst of his earthly
duties'. He is described as 'a regular worshipper at this
church for twenty six years during a great part of which he
read the lessons on Sundays.' He also 'served the district
faithfully for many years as an Alderman'. The memorial
concludes with the words from Tennyson's *In Memoriam*:

'God's finger touch'd him, and he slept.' His widow and his son, afterwards Sir Noel, stayed on for some years. Sir Alexander Carmichael Bruce, Assistant Commissioner of the Metropolitan Police for thirty years, until his retirement in 1914, lived for almost the whole of that period at No.82.

By 1878 Wyand the builder was living in one of his own houses at number 16 (later re-numbered 104). Edward Fox White, dealer in pictures, stayed on for years in the newly built number 57 (at first numbered 55). John Pickering, at No.110 (1879–1909), was a 'Railway Contractor employing 21 clerks'. A tablet in St Philip's Church recalls a man of that name, perhaps his father, as 'one of the earliest and liberal contributors to the building of this church' suggesting that the family had lived in the area long before Lexham Gardens was built. Edmund Foster at No.130 for ten years from 1879 was a Tea Merchant. Then at No.13 we find the Chairman of the Thames & Channel Steam Ship Company, so that commerce was represented.

However, perhaps the most interesting group among the early comers were those who were connected with the government of India. The first was Sir Cecil Beadon (No.4 re-numbered No. 92). He has been described as one of 'the two men with the most perfect manners'. Up the age of forty-five he had a brilliant career in India which was then blighted by a number of failures, partly caused by his ill health. He returned to London and spent his final years living here (1877–80).

Most distinguished of all was probably Lieutenant-General Sir Henry Norman. He lived at No.27 at the time of the Census of 1881, during a period of service in England when he was a member of the Council of India. He left to become Governor of Bermuda and then of Western Australia. The climax of his career came in 1893 when he accepted the appointment of Governor-General (Viceroy) of India, but declined it after a few days reflection on the grounds that his health was unlikely to remain strong enough for such a demanding post. He then lived in Cornwall Gardens, before becoming a Field Marshal and Governor of Chelsea Hospital which was especially built in the Seventeenth Century for retired soldiers and still continues in a splendid building set in its grounds. He died there in 1907. (See plate 8c.)

Norman was a veteran of the India Mutiny of 1857, and our early residents also included two of the bravest of the brave – holders of the Victoria Cross 'For Valour', won in those days. Lieut.-General J. J. M. Innes, at No.9 (1885–1902), of the Royal Engineers served as a young man throughout the Mutiny from the siege of Lucknow to Sultanpore where he won his award. He rose to become Inspector-General of Military Works in India. At No. 62 (1883–1893) lived General R. H. Keatinge who won the V.C. at the siege of Chandaire and also received the special thanks of the Governor-General. He was later Chief Commissioner in the Central Provinces and in Assam. The Indian Civil Service was also represented most eminently by Sir John Stracey, GCSI who was living at No.103 in 1881 though he was spending much time away in Italy, and by Sir Juland Danvers, KCSI at No.103 from 1882–1902. He had a long career in India in railways and Public Works, being also Chairman of the Bombay, Baroda and Central India Railway and the South Behar Railway Company.

There were other distinguished military officers: Surgeon General Currie at No.83 (1881–1897), General Thomas Stock at No.30 (in 1881), General William Corfield at No.128 (1879–83), Lt-General Craven Dickens at No.75 (1880–1897), General Sir Edward Williams at No.73 (1881–1906) Admiral Sir George Richards at No.56 (1883–1893), General Robert Maclagan and then General Sir Allen Johnson (1883–1905) at No.60, and a number of Colonels or their widows. General Johnson's family were remarkable in that he was one of nine brothers of a military family,

eight of whom became army officers and five of them
Generals. His nephew, Brigadier-General Sir Henry
Johnson, continued to occupy the house right through to
the 1940s.

Imperial service did not always lead to a comfortable
retirement in this prosperous part of London, a life of ease
and domestic happiness safe from sorrow. General W. P.
Tomkins, C.I.E., lived on into old age at No.120. A brass
by Cox and Buckley on the north wall of St Philip's
Church remembers his son:

> Captain William Edward Tomkins
> of the Royal Warwickshire Regiment
> and Indian Staff Corps
> who was killed in action
> at Markanai on the
> North West Frontier of India
> on 15th September 1897
> aged 30 years

The 'doyen of the Civil Service' when he retired after a
career lasting 50 years, Sir Arthur Guillum Scott lived at
No.41 from 1879–1909. His widow continued there for
many years afterwards. Diplomacy was represented by
Henry Howard, at No.85 in 1881 and at No.65 a few
years afterwards (1885–1895). He was later to be knighted
and ended a long career in the foreign service as British
Minister to the Vatican during the First World War.

Education was represented by A. J. B. Scott who ran a
school at No.1, and there was a Military Tutors at Nos.19
and 21 as early as 1881. This was the famous 'Jimmy's'
which later ran for many years at No.5. Mrs Frances
Hodgson Burnett bought No.44 around 1890 out of the
proceeds of her much criticized and very popular best
selling story, *Little Lord Fauntleroy* (1886). She let friends
run this as a boarding house for others including herself
(see Plate 8b.). Another Victorian writer, Mrs Mary

Louisa Molesworth, lived for a few years at No.85 at the end of the 1880s. She also wrote children's books.

Scholars were few. Edward Walker came to the newly finished No.59 (1879–1881) which was called Nayland House, and became No.61 in the re-numbering. His academic life began as a Fellow of Trinity College Cambridge, and he was by now a Fellow of the Royal Society. His noted work on *Terrestrial and Cosmical Magnetism* had been published in 1869.

A few clergymen, like Mr Claxton (see page 20 and Plate 8a.) also lived here, the most distinguished being the Right Reverend and Honourable Edward Stuart Talbot. He was contemporary with some of the younger of those men already mentioned, but he only came to live here at No. 45 in his retirement from 1925–34. The son of an Earl, he had been successively Bishop of Rochester, Southwark, and finally of Winchester. In 1915 his youngest son, Gilbert, was killed in action at Hooge, in Belgium, and at the end of the same year a soldiers' club was opened at Poperinghe, near Ypres. This was called Talbot House after him, and it was run by a remarkable young clergyman called 'Tubby' Clayton. In signalling, Talbot House was abbreviated to 'Toc H', and after the war Clayton established this in a wider way with a base in London. The movement spread throughout the Commonwealth as a meeting place for young men who were encouraged to spend some of their leisure time in the service of others.

It is fitting that the biographer of Queen Victoria and of her son, Edward VII, should have moved into No.108, though this was not until the 1890s. Sir Sidney Lee was also Assistant Editor, and then Editor of the *Dictionary of National Biography*. In this capacity he was responsible for the greater part of that work and the biographer of many individuals within it. He lived in Lexham Gardens from 1895 right on until this death in 1926. (See Plate 8a.)

Most of the houses were held leasehold at about £200 per annum, though a few were bought outright, like No.56 for which Admiral Richards paid £3,000. Nowadays, of course, a whole house would sell for over a million pounds. It is sometimes maintained that the central section, around the garden square, was socially superior, or that the north side of the western section and the south side of the garden square had mews accommodation behind them while the others did not. This is not so. Mews accommodation was simply taken up by those who needed it and could afford it, irrespective of which part of the road they lived in. Sidney Woolf, QC at No.101 clearly kept his brougham in the mews at the eastern end of the street.

The only noblemen to have live in Lexham Gardens seem to have been at the western end. The 3rd Earl of Stradbroke, of Henham Hall in Suffolk, and later Governor of Victoria, Australia, had his London residence at No.138 before the First World War, and the Earl of Shelburne, heir to the Marquess of Lansdowne, had a flat at No.99 in recent years. None of these, except perhaps Mrs Burnett, could be said to be 'household names' in their day, but nevertheless they do represent very solid professional standing.

Jimmy's

Future professional standing was also represented by what has been perhaps the most remarkable establishment in the history of Lexham Gardens – 'Jimmy's'. This was a private tutors or 'crammers' first founded elsewhere in 1864 by the Reverend Dr George Frost, to prepare young men for professional entrance. Frost had been for many years Chaplain at the Kensington Workhouse (later St Mary Abbots Hospital) and a master at the Grammar School. In 1880 these tutors were taken over and established in Lexham Gardens by Captain Walter Haweis James of the

Royal Engineers (see Plate 8d). Here they continued for the next ninety years, latterly under the name of Carlisle and Gregson and celebrating the centenary in 1964.

Captain James was already established at Nos. 19 and 21 Lexham Gardens by the time of the Census of April 1881 and his business later spread to Nos.5 & 7 also, eventually moving there altogether. He was soon joined by Captain Matthew Henry Gregson, and then in the 1890s by Edward Carlisle, a Cambridge Mathematician. At first 'Jimmy's' tutored only those who were preparing to compete for entry into the commissioned ranks of the British Army by way of the military academies at Sandhurst and Woolwich. This was through examination and the tutors prepared individuals for such papers. 'Jimmy's' soon became 'the most successful ... for the Sandhurst examination' among the 'crammers', and attracted many well connected young men, some of whom became extremely well-known. At the Centenary it was noted that among these were Prince Arthur of Connaught, the Duke of Norfolk, the Earl of Derby, Lord Ironside and Lord Gort, who were all very notable in their time. The fuller records of the business and its history would reveal many others.

However there was a pupil at 'Jimmy's' from March to June 1893 who was to become the most celebrated of them all, young Winston Churchill. His father, Lord Randolph Churchill, rather despaired of him and thought of sending him into the City to work in banking. His Head Master at Harrow persuaded the father to send him to Captain James instead to try again for the army. It is rather fascinating that James wrote these words from Lexham Gardens to Lord Randolph, about the future statesman. They also show 'Jimmy's' effective method of achieving success where others had failed:

> I have issued orders for your son to be kept at work and that in future he is to do the full hours. I had to speak to

him the other day about his casual manner. I think the boy means well but he is distinctly inclined to be inattentive and to think too much of his abilities. [He had been] rather inclined up to the present to teach his instructors instead of endeavouring to learn from them, and this is not the frame of mind conducive to success. [James concluded that young Winston had] suggested to me that his knowledge of history was such that he did not want any more teaching in it! ... this is problematical ... The boy has very many good points in him but what he wants is very firm handling.

Later, in *My Early Life*, Churchill self-deprecatingly recalled his three attempts to enter the Army.

When I had failed for the second time to pass into Sandhurst, I bade farewell to Harrow and was relegated as a forlorn hope to a 'crammer'. Captain James and his highly competent partners kept an establishment [off] the Cromwell Road. It was said that no one who was not a congenital idiot could avoid passing thence into the Army. The Firm had made a scientific study of the mentality of the Civil Service Commissioners. They knew with almost Papal infallibility the sort of questions which that sort of person would be bound on average to ask on any of the selected subjects. They specialised on these questions and on the answering of them. They fired a large number of efficient shot-guns into the brown of the covey, and they claimed a high and steady number of birds. Captain James – if he had known it – was really the ingenious forerunner of the inventors of the artillery barrages of the Great War. He fired from carefully selected positions upon the areas which he knew must be tenanted by large bodies of enemy troops. He had only to fire a given number of shells per acre per hour to get his bag. He did not need to see the enemy soldiers. Drill was all he had to teach his gunners. Thus year by year for at least two decades he held the Blue Ribbon among the Crammers. He was like one of those people who have a sure system for breaking the Bank of Monte Carlo, with the important difference that in a great

majority of cases his system produced success. Even the
very hardest cases could be handled. No absolute guarantee
was given, but there would always be far more than a
sporting chance.

Having suffered a serious accident, he recovered and with
the help of Captain James was successful in passing the
Army examination at the third attempt. (More than
seventy years later Churchill died, world renowned, only
half a mile away in another part of Kensington, 28 Hyde
Park Gate).

The compilers of the *Survey of London* provide us with
many fascinating details about this part of London, but
they made a major error over Captain James. Writing of
the social standing of early residents in Lexham Gardens
they observe that in 1881 one serving Captain in the
Royal Engineers, aged 33, had nine servants including a
butler and a footman to look after his family of six. This
is clearly a reference to James at No.19. They did not
note the small words inserted above his profession which
showed that he had retired from the army. Not only did
they omit to make any comment on the remarkable
history of 'Jimmy's' in this locality, or on James himself,
but they failed to realise that all these servants no doubt
also served the people who boarded next door at No.21.
They were all young men between 16 and 19 years of
age, and the first three listed were Lieutenants in militia
regiments. It was quite a common practice to obtain a
commission in the militia as a way of helping towards
gaining a place at military college and so achieving a
permanent career as an army officer. At the Census ten
years later (1891) 'Jimmy's' was firmly settled at Nos. 5 and
7, but Captain James was living with his family at No.57,
(see below page 57) with a more reasonable entourage of
only six servants: a butler, a cook, a footman, two house-
maids and a kitchen maid.

When Carlisle and Gregson closed, the houses at Nos. 5

& 7 were demolished to make way for the new building housing the Yugoslavian Embassy, a prophetic end in view of the tragic break up of that country twenty years later.

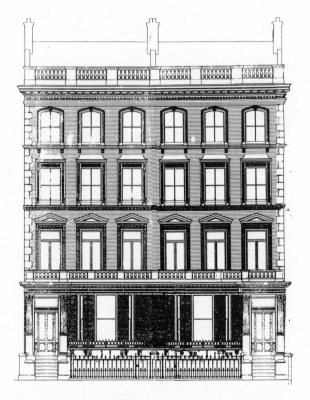

Nos. 5 & 7 Lexham Gardens (now demolished);
long associated with 'Jimmy's' (Carlisle and Gregson),
No.5 for more than for more than eighty years.

3

A Victorian Childhood in Lexham Gardens

Son of a Rising Barrister

Leonard Woolf (1880–1969), publisher, writer, Socialist, and eventually the husband of the famous writer Virginia Woolf, was already living at No.101 Lexham Gardens at the Census of 1881. He was then aged five months. His father, Sidney Woolf, whose death in 1892 led to the family having to leave this 'white elephant of a house' for the comparative poverty of a detached house in Putney, was a barrister and soon to become a Queen's Counsel, making 'I believe, over £5,000 a year.' Woolf remembers these early years with considerable affection. (Plate 16.)

'To a Londoner the rhythm of London traffic is part of the rhythm of his blood and of his life. I was born to the rhythm of horses' hooves in broughams, hansom cabs, and fourwheelers clattering down London streets, and body and blood have never completely synchronised their beat to the whir and roar and hoot of cars. One of my earliest recollections is of lying in bed high up in a front room of the house in Lexham Gardens, night after night, listening to the clop, clop, clop of a horse in a carriage or hansom cab break the silence of the night as it came down the street past our house. Clop, clop, clop – somehow or other that noise from outside gave a sense of security, stability as one hugged oneself together under the bedclothes'. (See Plate 14b.)

We would love to know more. Nonetheless he ranges over some interesting features from such a childhood: the nursery, sickness, the garden, his father, early fears, and reactions in later years to the worth of it all.

The Nursery

'My nurse, who was with us for many years and brought us all up, had much less education than our governesses, but she was the first person to interest me in books and in the strange and fascinating workings of the human mind ... I can still feel myself physically enfolded in the warmth and safety of the great nursery on the third floor of the house in Lexham Gardens, the fire blazing behind the tall guard, the kettle singing away, and nurse, with her straight black hair parted in the centre ... so the nursery with its great fire, when the curtains were pulled and the gas lit and nurse settled down to her reading, and occasionally far off could be heard the clop-clop of a horse in a hansom cab or four-wheeler, the nursery remains for me the Platonic idea laid up in heaven of security and peace and civilisation. But though in the course of my life I have passed through several desolations of desolation more desolate than the garden with its grimy ivy and its spider webs, I never again found any safety and civilisation to equal that of the gas-lit nursery.'

Early fears

'Outside the security of that nursery, terrible and terrifying things happened in Kensington and London. Hushed or whispered stories of Jack the Ripper, I think penetrated into the nursery, and in my schoolroom days we were all terrified by a little woman, dressed all in black, who on foggy winter nights lurked in the Kensington streets, stabbed unsuspecting gentlemen with a long knife, and then disappeared into the darkness and the fog ...'

Illness

He recalls having a very severe attack of scarlet fever and 'a man coming into the room and applying leeches to my back. I insisted upon seeing the leeches and was fascinated by them ... At one moment my illness took a turn for the worse and I was, so it was said, upon the point of death. They called in Sir William Jenner, the Queen's doctor [descended from the Dr Jenner who is so famously connected with small-pox] ... He was a kindly man and I was fascinated by the shape of his nose.' When asked if he would like something now, young Woolf was to 'remember looking carefully into his kindly old face and saying: I should like to pull your nose.' And pull it he did.

The Garden

'Behind the house in Lexham Gardens was a long parallelogram enclosed by the house on the north and on the other three sides by three grimy six-foot walls. It was a typical London garden of that era, consisting of a worn parallelogram of grass surrounded by narrow gravel paths and then narrow beds of sooty, sour London soil against the walls. Each child was given a few feet of bed for his own personal "garden" and there we sowed seeds or grew pansies bought off barrows in the Earl's Court Road. I was very fond of my "garden" ...'.

Sunday and his father

'It was on my seventh or eighth birthday that [my father] gave me a tricycle — it was the days before the "safety" bicycle was invented, and he and my elder brother, Herbert, already each had their tricycle. On Sunday we all three set off together on our tricycles from Lexham Gardens, along Hammersmith Road, across the Bridge to Barnes Common, to Sheen and Richmond Park ...

Sunday lunch was a ceremony of some importance, for the whole family, capable of sitting upright and of eating

roast beef, sat round the table. I suppose that in the house in Lexham Gardens towards the end of the 1880s six of the nine children sat round the table at Sunday lunch with my father and mother. There was always an immense sirloin of beef, carved with considerable ceremony by my father ...'
Then 'in the 1880s a Victorian lunch in a Victorian family like the Woolfs was a formidable, but not altogether unpleasant ritual. It was eminently bourgeois, patriarchal, and a weekly apotheosis of the family. The change from the matriarchy of weekdays to the patriarchy of Sundays was very impressive to a small boy, and to me it was very sympathetic. My father practically never stopped working ... After dinner and on Saturdays, if he was at home, he worked on his briefs. In the week therefore I saw very little of him. Sometimes, I was allowed to go into his dressing room before breakfast to see him shaved, and sometimes my mother took me in the brougham to fetch him from the Temple ...'

Behaviour
'The standard of behaviour, what was expected of a "little gentleman" or a "little lady" by nurses and governesses in the 1880s in Lexham Gardens, was pretty high.'

Games
'At home we used to play cricket for hours in the back garden with a tennis ball and elaborate rules for scoring runs. My eldest brother, Herbert, and I developed very early a passion for bicycling. He must have been about twelve and I eleven when he acquired on his birthday his first bicycle. It was before the days of pneumatic tyres and we took the incredibly heavy and clumsy machine out into Lexham Gardens in order to acquire the art of riding. After a few minutes' practice he allowed me to try my hand, or rather legs. The seat was too high for me and I went off with great speed along the gutter, such speed indeed that I

collided violently with a lamp post and the bicycle split in two, the handlebars and front wheel going in one direction, the back wheel, seat, and myself in another. Later we became experts ...' and he goes on to describe tours as far away as the Shetlands.

Money and security

'Before my father died, I ... had a profound and, of course, completely unconscious sense of economic security, and, therefore, personally of social security. Money was not talked about or thought about or worried about; it was just there to be spent, not recklessly or extravagantly, but on things which ladies and gentlemen needed or wanted. And the social background, the house and servants and brougham and Sunday sirloin, which were based upon this invisible and unmentioned money, were accepted without question as stable and permanent, like the money.'

Retrospect from later years

'I think that there was something to be said for the kind of life lived by the Victorian Woolf family in Lexham Gardens and by the many other similar bourgeois families in Bayswater and Kensington ... I have been a Socialist for most of my life. But the social standards of value in Lexham Gardens were very high, much higher than in any proletarian society ... There is much that can be and has been legitimately said against family life on the grand scale, as developed by the middle classes of the nineteenth century: its snugness and smugness, snobbery, its complacent exploitation of economic, sexual, and racial classes ... Yet it also had high psychological and aesthetic values ... The actual relations between the human beings living in these large households related by blood or friendship were, on the whole, in my remembrance extraordinarily human and humane ...'

4

Lexham Gardens Houses

The Builders

First to build was John Sprake, who had recently constructed the eighty foot wide Cromwell Road extension for Lord Kensington and two other landowners. Between 1872–75 he was responsible for a block of fourteen houses on the north side of the west end of Lexham Road, those which are numbered 120–146. More important for us, and for the whole of Lexham Gardens, was Samuel Juler Wyand. He first built a block of eight houses on the north side. These were numbers 90–104, and building was begun in 1874. They stand immediately opposite Lee Abbey which occupies the houses numbered 57–67. Wyand lived in No. 104, one of the first of the houses he built here, for nearly forty years from 1876. A year later he added Numbers 106 and 108. These concluded his terrace of ten houses. In the same period, 1876–77, James Whitaker built numbers 110–118, on ground originally assigned to Sprake and with those already erected by him and those now finished by Wyand, the whole of the north side from Earl's Court Road to Marloes Road was complete. Wyand had previously begun building in this immediate area at the beginning of 1872 with the four short terraces in Marloes Road, on either side of the street openings into what was shortly to be developed as Lexham Gardens.

Very soon after building his first block on the north side

of Lexham Road, Wyand commenced the row of ten houses opposite. These were numbered 57–75, where building began in 1875, and was completed over the next four years. Wyand built up the remainder of the south side of this stretch of the street between 1875–79. The first six (numbers 77–87) to be added to the original ten were of similar height and design. The remaining nine (numbers 89–105) were smaller, with only four main storeys and these have white brick facades with stuccoed dressings, instead of fully stuccoed fronts. Unity in the whole side of the street is maintained only in the Doric porticoes (though not all are of the same width) and in the ironwork. This makes the joining of the porticoes of Nos.59 and 61 to make the main entrance to Lee Abbey particularly offensive, and it is the Warden's hope that restoration can be attempted soon.

The western end of Lexham Gardens generally survives intact as it was built, and fortunately there was no serious war damage.

Looking at the eastern side of Marloes Road, the principal builder was Wyand, but he was not the first. He was possibly delayed by decisions which led to the garden square being adopted as a welcome variation in the design (see above – page 16). Starting at the extreme east end, the firm of Stevens and Colls were responsible for numbers 1–7 and 2–10 in 1875–77. These survive, with the exception of Nos. 5 and 7 which were demolished to enable the new Yugoslavian Embassy to be built in 1972–75.

Most of the remaining south side was also constructed in 1875–77 by two builders. William Ashfold was responsible for numbers 19–29, and also numbers 20–34 on the eastern side of the curve into Cromwell Road, during 1875–76. George Edward Mineard built the rest of the south side, numbers 31–55. Five of these, numbers 45–53, were bombed during the Second World War. The red-brick block of flats, Lexham House, replaced them.

With the south side completed by 1877, there remained two sections to be filled in. On the east curve, William Henry Willis completed both sides with numbers 9–17 and 12–18 during 1877–78. There remained much of the northern side lying to the east of Marloes Road (see page 18).

Wyand began to build the more northerly line of houses in 1877, and in 1878 the whole of the street was renamed Lexham Gardens. Altogether Wyand took seven years to complete his houses, and they fill the north side completely, numbers 40–44 and 48–88. There remained only one small area of land in the north–east corner of the development. It may be that a road was planned to link up with Cornwall Gardens further to the east. In the event William Douglas built two houses there in 1882–84, numbered 36 and 38, and he also constructed Lexham Gardens Mews to the north of No.38. With the completion of the various mews the development was finished.

The House that Never Was

Careful readers will have noted that No.46 is omitted from the summary so far. Why was it never built? Wyand had secured all the plots on that stretch of the north side of Lexham Road to the east of Marloes Road. The last of his houses to be built there were Nos.40–44 which faced the garden in the north-east corner. They were completed in 1884. This area was somewhat contentious owing to the problem of making an access through to Cornwall Gardens and the problem of the railway in that area. With the building of Nos.36 and 38 and the laying out of Lexham Gardens Mews in 1882–84 only the plot of No.46 remained as a possible way through to the east. There was much local agitation for this. However, both the freeholder, Lord Kensington and the leaseholder, Wyand, refused to give up the site. The Kensington parish Vestry carried on a long campaign and finally both agreed to receive compensation in return for surrendering their rights, Wyand obtaining no less than £1,150. Lexham Walk was made in 1887 as a walk-way only through to Cornwall Gardens. The houses which are now Nos.1 and 3 Lexham Walk were not built until 1909–10, and were first called Nos.46 and 46a Lexham Gardens, but Wyand's No.46 never materialised. (See Plate 14a.)

Who Designed the Houses?

This seems a very natural question to ask in the 1990s, but less so of the 1870s.

> The basic job of architects representing freeholders of building land was to act as their estate surveyors. This position was normally held throughout the nineteenth century by men who conceived their profession to be that of surveyor as much as architect. The scope of such employment depended both upon a landowner's wishes and upon the powers and policies of his other crucial representative, his lawyer.

Martin Joseph Stutely had certainly been designing buildings and acting as an architect before he became surveyor to the second Lord Kensington around 1844. He held this position for the next thirty five years under the third and fourth barons and was succeeded about 1880 by his son-in-law, Daniel Cubitt Nichols. Nichols favoured the 'new red brick architecture' which first appeared on the Edwardes estate in 1880 in Nevern Square under the architect Walter Graves, but this was too late to affect Lexham Gardens.

There were various ways in which the surveyor might influence the architecture. In one of these

> the surveyor settled layouts of the land, sent them to the Metropolitan Board of Works for approval, scrutinized the plans of builders and others, and probably stipulated certain

facing materials mentioned in the building agreements; yet the evidence of strong architectural intervention in the estate's appearance is lacking. This kind of remit many have been the commonest in the mid Victorian period. It appears to have been the method of working on the Edwardes estate after the 1840s during the surveyorship of M. J. Stutely and Daniel Cubitt Nichols ...

If Stutely was not a major influence in the design of the houses (see also pages 98 and 103), we must turn our attention to the speculative builders.

The commonest involvement for the architect in speculative housing was, indeed, as a subordinate to the developer-builder. As the role was professionally inglorious it was little talked about, so that the normal conditions and divisions of responsibility are far from clear. But it may be hazarded that after about 1850, when houses grew larger, more intricate and more ambitious, at least the elevations and to some extent the plans of most houses in Southern Kensington emanated from an architectural office of some sort.

In Wyand's case there seems to be no record of the identity of the architect for the reasons just given. It is known that Wyand employed the architect George Devey to provide schemes for interior embellishment of No.65 and possibly other houses around 1885, presumably when he was fitting them out for new occupiers. He certainly used Devey to design houses in parts of Chelsea at that time, but there is no evidence of his employment of him earlier. The architect Henry Godwin clearly produced a layout for Nos.36 and 38 built by William Douglas, and laid out Lexham Gardens Mews in 1882–84, but even this is not evidence that he was the designer of the houses themselves. Halsey Ricardo designed a loggia for (Sir) Juland Danvers when he moved in to No.103 in 1881. Nothing more definite seems to be available about the architects who worked for the other builders here.

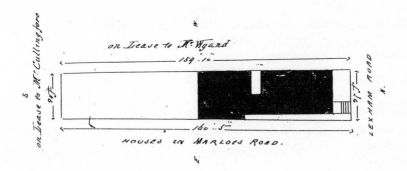

Ground plan of No.57 from the Indenture

The papers in the Middlesex Deeds Registry include the Indentures from William, Lord Kensington leasing to the builder. These have a ground plan attached. Sometimes this simply gives the dimension of the plot of land, as in the case of No.67. At best the outline of the building is also marked as with No.57 illustrated above. It clearly shows the light well. The frontage here is 27 ft. but for this type of house by Wyand it was usually 22 ft. This Indenture is dated 4th June 1875. The plan is reduced, and reprinted by permission of the Greater London Records Office (microfilm X73/1532).

The Lexham Gardens Houses (Builders and External Details)

The whole of Lexham Gardens was built between 1872–84 by eight different builders. All the houses were in conventional late-Italianate terrace style, even when they were built detached like No.55.

Not everyone will be interested in the details of architecture and style. This information is given in the Appendix at the end of the book (see pages 91–101).

Lexham Gardens Houses (Interiors)

It is still possible to see what the interior of a Kensington house of this period really looked like. Linley Sambourne House, at 18 Stafford Terrace, two streets behind the Safeway on Kensington High Street, was completed in 1873. It was bought a year later by E. L. Sambourne on a lease of 89 years for £2,000. With his wife he then set about the furnishing and decorations which are substantially the same today. The house remained in the family, and it was opened by the Victorian Society as a museum in 1980.

At the close of the Nineteenth Century the German Embassy in London had a new additional member of staff. Hermann Muthesius was appointed to study and report on English Architecture. This he did in his *Das Englische Haus* published in Germany in 1904–05. He analysed the situation which he found here, criticising and assessing, and inevitably comparing Britain with Germany, not always to the advantage of his own country. He spotted the fact that

> the normal town-house ... that occurs all over England is the terrace-house. Its street frontage measures between 6 and 9 meters and it is usually built in long, uniform rows, the effect of which in most cases is weary in the extreme. This is true even of the best quarters in which people who keep horses and carriage live ... Nevertheless, one will find few of the excesses of jerry building and tastelessness that we know so well from the tenement houses of Berlin ... this partly reconciles one to the lack of intelligence apparent elsewhere.

He also observed that

> The basic form of the house has remained constant for a hundred and fifty years: it is a six storeyed, extremely narrow-fronted terrace-house, entirely lacking in individuality. The architecture of the exterior does not usually vary between one house and the next, their facades run on with

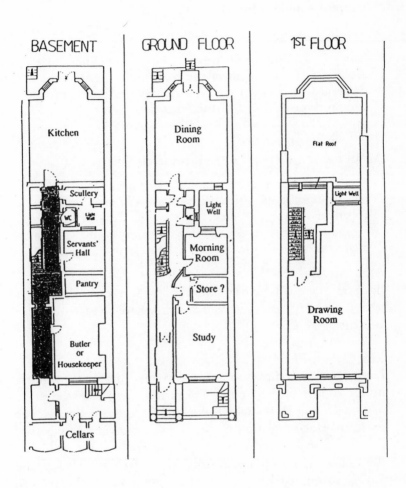

From the Estate Agents' brochures of twenty or thirty years later it is possible to reconstruct what a sale advertisement **might have looked like** for one of Wyand's houses (such as No. 67) at the time of building (*see pages 53–54*). Read it in conjunction with this plan which has been put together from existing plans of the Lee Abbey houses, and the description on page 42–47. See also the plan on page 48.

the same features to the point at which the developer has staked the limit of his plot.

Muthesius also grasped the interior lay-out:

The ground-plans of the urban terrace-house differ slightly according to the depth of the blocks, but on the whole, especially in regard to the distribution of rooms on the various floors, there is a basic, unchanging form.

The Semi-Basement:
Again the same writer introduces us to this:

The domestics offices in the basement occupy every inch of available space, which, as we have seen, extends to the cellars under the pavement ... Since the English see it as the butler's place to sleep beside his pantry so that he may guard the silver, his room is in the basement.

Alternatively, this room was for the Housekeeper. On this floor also would be the kitchen, with range, dressers, a larder, scullery, and a servants' hall where they would eat, and their W. C.

The Ground Floor
Here, and on the floor above, would be the principal public rooms of the house. Taken in order these were:

The *Dining Room* which was on the ground floor at the back, overlooking the garden, and was conveniently placed for food to be served from the kitchen below, accessible up the stairs which opened onto the corridor outside the dining room. At Lee Abbey this stair is still to be seen in Nos.57 and 61, but in No.67 this has since been reversed.

The *Morning Room* was in the middle of the ground floor with a window on to the light well. Sometimes it had a pleasing stained glass window which gave light, but obscured the dull and viewless aspect. At Lee Abbey the best preserved of these is at No.61 recently used as the office for Accommodation or Accounts. Satisfying a Victorian enjoyment of romantic nostalgia, there is on the right a bearded cavalier. To the left we see this charmingly painted lady of uncertain historical costume, her face framed in a veil.

Portrait in a stained glass window of the Morning Room at No. 61.

This room was for the personal use of the lady of the house. It would have been much easier to heat that the vast sitting room on the first floor, and here she could entertain friends. In this boudoir she could write letters or sew, give orders to the servants for the daily tasks and write out the menus for the meals. It was usually very comfortably furnished and was likely to be well decorated with family photographs as well as other mementos of a personal and more intimate nature. House-plants might also be very much in evidence.

The *Study* occupied the front of our houses and had a masculine purpose. Depending on the interests of the master of the house it could be used as a study, as in the case of practising lawyers like Sidney Woolf, as a library for those who were retired or who had scholarly interests, or as a billiard room. Muthesius points out 'there is always a cloak-room and a men's lavatory as well' on this floor.

It is interesting that he makes no mention of the hall which in many Victorian houses was such an important feature. Many callers would gain no further access, never penetrating in beyond the glass doors set back in our case a dozen feet behind the front door (and still to be seen at Nos.57 and 67). These divided the inner and the outer halls, the latter providing an effective ante-chamber in which a servant could say politely that master or mistress was not at home. The tessellated tiled floor (still mainly there at Nos.57 and 67, and hopefully to be restored) stretched from the front door throughout the corridor to the doorway of the Dining Room. (The corridor is still complete at No.57.)

The First Floor:
Muthesius continues:

> The *drawing-room* is on the first floor; in accordance with an old tradition it is a "double drawing-room", i.e. either two rooms one behind the other joined by a wide archway, or a large room of some other shape, such as an L-shape.

Such was the case in our houses. Photographs survive of the L-shaped drawing room of No.32 in 1907 (see Plate 7). Drawing Rooms in the Lee Abbey houses were similar, occupying the whole of the first floor of the house. Three long French casement windows opened onto a balcony at the front. The ceiling was divided into three sections. The first occupied the whole width of the house. It was divided at the point where the doorway led out into the corridor and stair case. The second was a square adjacent to the corridor or landing. Both of these had a deep and ornate cornice, similar to those on the ground floor rooms. The third section was above a small area in front of the rear window, over-hanging the light well. This was possibly enclosed with a glass screen, which formed a conservatory attracting the warmth and light of the south facing aspect.

> A large house will probably have another room for the women of the house on this floor, as well as a bedroom with communicating dressing-room and bath for visitors. The *second floor* is the main bedroom floor. The main staircase ascends to this floor, if as is sometimes the case, it has not been terminated at the first floor.
>
> The *third floor* is reserved for the children: there will be a large day-nursery facing south if possible), two or three bedrooms, a bath, lavatory, store-room, linen-cupboard, etc. The *fourth floor* is occupied by servants' bedrooms and possibly spare-rooms; here also is the storage tank for the house and a fire-exit ... Thus the characteristic ground-plan of the larger English terrace-house has evolved and the sequence of rooms is broken in the centre by the introduction of a light-well, by means of which light and air are brought into the centre of the house; it also provides an opportunity of lighting the main and the services staircases, both of which adjoin the light-well. All the ancillary rooms, such as the lavatories, bathrooms, cloakrooms etc. are grouped round the light-well, thus enabling them to be fitted comfortably into the ground-plan.

The Way of Life in These Houses

We have seen that those who came to live in Lexham Gardens belonged to the prosperous upper middle classes

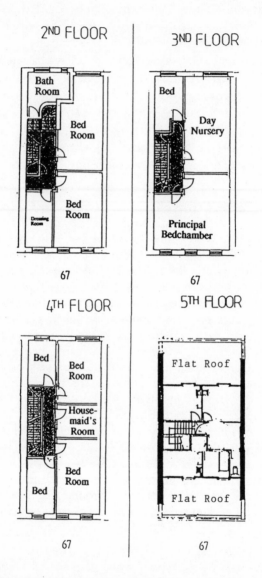

Read pages 46–47 in conjunction with this. Sometimes there was a fifth floor, as in these houses. Here the plan is not accurate for the services, storage and servants. See the caption on page 43.

of Victorian society. In a day when a working wage might be £50 a year, it required a really good income to lease a house for £200 a year, furnish it, and maintain a suitable life-style with servants. Husbands would spend much of their time away from home working in the law courts or Government departments, or if they were retired, at the Club in Piccadilly or St James's. In contrast wives did not go out to work, but ran the home, entertained, and managed the children.

The Census returns for 1881, at which time not all the houses had yet been completed, give a good account of a typical household. This was staffed by an average of five servants each. These would include a butler, or a house-keeper, a footman, a cook, a lady's maid, a parlourmaid, a housemaid, a kitchen maid, a governess, or a nurse, depending on the family circumstances. The senior servant would keep the accounts for the household and these would be checked regularly by the master. A typical servant's wage would be £20 a year, but in addition they would receive free lodging and meals. These would be taken in the basement of the house with the other servants. The family would eat on the ground floor and be waited on there.

In 1881 No.87 was in charge of a housekeeper. Nos.7 and 71 had Police Constables living in them, perhaps because their wives were in charge, and No.136 had a Chelsea pensioner whose wife was the caretaker. Such instances may have been between owners, or because the family was away at the time.

The family lived on the ground floor, on the first and second floors, with the children on the third floor. The servants lived and worked in the basement or at the top of the house. In grander houses than these there would have been a separate staircase, so that the family would not be meeting the servants about their work. This was not so here. Originally our houses would not have had hot running water. This would have to be carried up stairs by the servants as would coal for the fires in every room. The Drawing Room might have had two fire-places. With so many rooms and floors it was important to be able to call servants easily when needed. There was a system of hand-bells which rang in the basement when a handle was turned in a room occupied by a member of the family. There was also likely to be a speaking tube connecting the dining room with the kitchen below, and perhaps other rooms. By blowing down the tube a whistle sounded which attracted a servant who would then come and take the message through the earpiece.

The Social Scene

We have seen that the original inhabitants belonged to the professional or leisured upper middle classes. In some parts of Kensington this social atmosphere soon degenerated, especially where it became difficult to dispose of new houses. This was not true in Lexham Gardens where many of the original families remained for thirty or forty years. Even the appalling upheaval of the First World War did not destroy the early atmosphere. Around that time more retired Colonial servants acquired houses here, including Sir Everard im Thurn (at No.39 from about 1911) who had been Governor of Fiji, Sir William Ovens Clark (No.43 from about the same time) who had been Chief Justice of the Punjab, Sir James Shaw Hay (No.42 1905–24) who had been Governor of Sierre Leone and then of Barbados until his retirement in 1900. Amongst others there were Sir Howland Roberts, Bt. (No.75a 1910–17 with his widow continuing) and Judge James Rentoul at No.44 (1910–1920). If some of these only stayed a few years, others took their places.

In the 1920s and 1930s there was still Bishop Talbot, and then his widow at No.45, as we have seen, preceded there by Sir Hoyle Howarth (from about 1913 until his death in 1923.) Sir Herbert Stephen (Viginia Woolf's cousin) was at No.144 for several years from 1915. Sir Lindsey Smith (No.68 from about 1920–60) who had been Chief Justice of Zanzibar, continued there until his death despite the destruction of No.66 in 1940. Lady Mary Bridgeman was at No.37 in her widowhood from about 1915–38, at first accompanied by her sister, Lady Susan Fortescue, daughters of the 3rd Earl Fortescue. Next door, at No.35 was Matilda, Lady Williams. Her three sons in turn succeeded their father in the baronetcy, the last being killed-in-action at the age of eighteen. The Revd Charles Moor, DD came to No.14 after retiring as Vicar of Gainsborough in 1901, the year before his forty-fifth birthday. Soon after that he published *A History of Gainsborough*, and lived on into his old age here until the 1930s. Vice-Admiral Sir Robert Mansell spent his retirement as Deputy Master of Trinity House while living at No.69 until 1936. Brigadier General Alfred Huggins was at No.91; the Guillum Scotts were still at No.41 in the 1930s; Sir Henry Johnson continued at No.60 into the 1940s, and there was a fair sprinkling of retired naval officers and Colonels and Majors well beyond the first fifty years of occupation.

This is not to deny that some houses were being divided into flats when large numbers of servants were no longer being kept. This reflected social and economic changes, but did not necessarily mean that the standing of the residents had lowered greatly before 1940.

Domestic and Non-Domestic Housing

There is an assumption that the traditional use for the Lexham Gardens houses was family occupation. While this is largely true for the earliest period it is not entirely so. Even then there were schools at Nos.1 and 65 and an Army tutors at Nos.19 & 21, 5 & 7. The first occupier of Nos.36–38, H.

B. Lewis, had them joined internally from the start and the assumption must be that this was for commercial purposes. For the first ten years of their life the builder, Wyand, seems to have used Nos.90–94 as a store.

If we consider more certain non-domestic occupation, No.52 was the Swiss Legation for about ten years from before 1895. Soon after the start of the twentieth century Nos.4 & 6, and very quickly No.8 also, became the Imperial Social (Professional Gentlewomen's) Club. By then Nos.34–38 were certainly a private hotel, and Nos.19 & 21 a boarding house possibly still connected with 'Jimmy's', run first by Miss Haynes and then by Miss Villiers. From 1910 Nos.57, 59, 61, and 63 were in commercial use as we shall soon see. At the end of the First World War No.71 was Queen Mary's Emergency Hostel. During that War Mrs Wilkins opened No.116 as a boarding house, and with Nos.112 & 114 this soon became the Lexham Gardens Hotel. In the 1920s it must have been somewhat confusing to have this so named, together with the Lexham Mansions Hotel, which is what Nos.34–38 were now called, and the Lexham Court Hotel (see below, page 60). By this time Mrs Goldsmith was running Nos.1 & 3 as a private hotel also. Before the Second World War Nos.17–21 had become Ye Hostelry Ladies' Hotel, Nos.62 & 66 the Lexham Private Hotel, Nos. 71 and 73 the Alexa Hotel, and No.32 was added to Nos.34–38. These last houses were taken over in that War as the Canadian Young Men's Christian Association, and by 1945 there were also some boarding houses and a guest house in this road.

It is a little difficult to understand those who favour a complete return to domestic occupation. Nowadays that means dividing houses into several flats, which in turn means heavy motorisation and pressures on parking. In contrast, non-domestic occupation reduces greatly such environmental problems.

PLATE 1a. No. 146 by Sprake; the first house, begun 1872.

PLATE 1b. Wyand porticoes and terraces; nos. 67–73 seen through No. 90.

PLATE 1c. No. 85 by Wyand, 1875–79 with less depth than in Nos. 57–75.

PLATE 1d. No. 105 by Wyand, 1878.

PLATE 2a. No. 108 by Wyand –
without the top storey.

PLATE 2b. Nos. 20–22 by
Ashfold, 1875–76.

PLATES 2c. and d. Mineard's terrace seen through the Gardens, and
No. 55 detached originally for a road through to the left.

PLATE 3a. No. 110 by Whitaker, and the best preserved.

PLATE 3b. Nos. 2–10: stucco and iron by Stevens and Colls 1875–77.

PLATE 3c. Lexham Gardens Mews, the shortest of the three opening off Lexham Gardens.

PLATE 4a. Nos. 12–14 by W. H. Willis, 1877–78.

PLATE 4b. Nos. 17–23, by Willis and Ashfold.

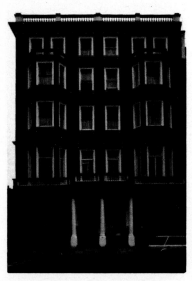

PLATE 4c. Nos. 36–38 by Douglas, 1882–84.

PLATE 4d. Nos. 5 and 7 demolished for a new Yugoslav Embassy.

PLATE 5a. Nos. 45–53, demolished after war damage; rebuilt as Lexham House, ameliorated here by trees.

PLATE 5b. No. 66 rebuilt after war damage, another storey within it.

PLATE 5c. Turning the corner: Nos. 25 and 27 by Ashfold 1875–76.

PLATE 6a. Nos. 44 and 48–74 Lexham Gardens
from a postcard of 1903.
(Courtesy of the Kensington and Chelsea Library)

PLATE 6b. A similar view today.

PLATE 7. The Edwardes Estate: A typical L-shaped Drawing Room on the first floor of No. 32 Lexham Gardens in 1907 when occupied by F. G. Adcock, Esq., William Ashfold, builder 1875–76.
(By Courtesy of The National Monuments Record)

Early residents in Lexham Gardens

PLATE 8   a. The Revd Joseph Claxton, first to arrive at No. 1 (now No. 146);   b. Frances Hodgson Burnett with her London home at No. 44, 1889–92;   c. General Sir Henry Norman 'a fine old warrior with delightful manners and an agreeable smile' at No. 27; d. Captain Walter James *(R.E. Museum)* tutored Winston Churchill at No. 5;   e. Sir Sidney Lee wrote his biographies from No. 108.

PLATE 9. No. 50 viewed behind the summer house.

PLATE 10a. The View from Ley Manor, later re-built as Lee Abbey.

PLATE 10b. Lee Abbey near Lynton, North Devon.

Lee Abbey in Courtfield Gardens.

PLATE 11   a. Melbourne,   b. Courtfield,   c. Edinburgh,   d. Sedan
– the house on the left with St Jude's Church on the right.

PLATE 12a. The Suncourt Hotel looking rather sanitised on this post-card used by guests.

PLATE 12b. The Hotel's Dining Room about 1980.

PLATE 13a. Announcing the move to
Lexham Gardens, September 1982.

PLATE 13b. Bishop Wakeling and Lord Belstead
chatting at the official opening.

PLATE 14a. Four heavy ornamental iron posts by Nowell & Robson (1887) in front of Lexham Walk, where No. 46 was never built.

PLATE 14b. A pub sign in nearby Earl's Court road evokes the 1880s.

PLATE 14c. Heavily shrouded No. 78 was saved from demolition in 1995.

PLATE 15a. Nos. 110–146 on the north west.

PLATE 15b. Nos. 4–18 on the east side of the curve.

PLATE 16. This portrait of Leonard Woolf (1880–1969) is by his sister-in-law, Vanessa Bell, and shows him as he may have looked when writing his reminiscences of childhood in Lexham Gardens. *(By courtesy of The National Portrait Gallery, London)*

PARTICULARS

The Substantially-built,
Light, Airy, and Well-fitted TOWN RESIDENCE

Known as

No. 67, Lexham Gardens, Kensington, W.

Situated in a central and open part of this Fashionable
Residential District, well removed from the noise of traffic,
yet within five minutes' walk of Kensington High Street, one of
London's finest shopping centres, with Railway Stations there
and at Earl's Court (constant service of trains by the District
Railway and the Brompton and Piccadilly Tube), close to several
Omnibus routes, within an easy walk of Kensington Gardens, the
Albert Hall, the Museums, Science and Art Schools, and Pro-
Cathedral.

**NOTE. Street Organs and Bands are expressly prohibited from
playing in Lexham Gardens.**

The Property commands a frontage of about 22 ft., with an elevation of imposing character in brick and stucco facings, and wide
entrance portico. A tiled **Vestibule** opens by screen doors to the
wide **Inner Hall**, with tessellated floor, and thence to

A Lofty and well proportion Dining Room,
with bay window, about 26 ft. (in bay) by 20 ft. and fitted
stove, with tiled hearth and enamelled slate mantel.

A Morning Room,
about 12 ft. by 9 ft. with register stove and marble mantel.

A Capital Library,
about 14 ft. 6 ins. by 20 ft. 6 ins. with tiled register stove
and marble mantel. At the end of the hall there is a **Gentleman's
Cloak Cupboard**; also W.C. with lavatory basin. China closet. A
wide stone Staircase, with ornamental iron balusters leads to

The Handsome Double Drawing Room,
about 43 ft. by 20 ft. wide in front portion. This is a very
lofty room and has these casements opening to a stone **Balcony**.
It is fitted with oak parquet floor, two stoves, with tiled
hearths and richly carved marble mantels; also a large mirror.
The centre of the room is divided by a wide Moorish arch. At the
rear (south facing) window there is a very attractive
Conservatory having tiled floor, and fitted with rockeries, fish
pond and fountain.

There is a W.c. and a lavatory on the half-landing.

Reconstruction of a Sale Advertisment c. 1878 (see page 43).

On the Second floor:

One or Two principal Bedrooms and a Dressing Room,
about 25 ft. by 11 ft., 18ft. by 11 ft. and 13 ft. 6 ins. by 7 ft. 6
ins., each fitted slow combustion stoves and marble mantels.
(Alternatively one Principal Bedchamber, about 20 ft. by 18 ft.
lighted by three windows, and one Principal Bedroom, about 25 ft. by
11 ft.). Two cupboards on the landing. Bathroom with fitted bath.

On the Third floor are:

Two Large Bedrooms and two other bedrooms,
about 25 ft. by 11 ft. (also suitable as Day Nursery), 18 ft. by 11
ft., 13 ft. 6 ins. by 7 ft. 6 ins, and 8 ft. by 7 ft. 6 ins. respectively each fitted slow combustion stove.

On the Fourth floor are:

Four Other Bedrooms
about 18 ft. by 11 ft., 14 ft. 6 ins by 11 ft., 13 ft. 6 ins. by 7
ft. 6 ins, and 8 ft. by 7 ft. 6 ins. respectively each fitted slow
combustion stove.

Housemaid's room about 11 ft. by 10 ft., and cupboard.

On the Fifth floor:

Services, servants's rooms or storage.

In the basement:

The Domestic Offices are ample for a large staff of servants, and
comprise **Large Airy Kitchen**, with a bay window, fitted kitchener,
with two ovens, dresser, hot plate, and store cupboard, Larder and
Scullery with tiled floor and glazed sink. Two coal cellars and W.C.;
also large wine cellar and wide passage. **Servants' Hall** with stove,
enamelled slate mantel, linen press, and drawers and cupboard.
Butler's Pantry, with fire-place, sink and china and glass cupboard.
Boot and knife house. Tradesman's Entrance.

Drainage on Modern Principles - Gas Light is installed.

Electric bells and Speaking Tubes are fitted.

There is a pleasant Garden in the rear, about 80 ft long by 21 ft
6 ins. wide.

The Residence is of the Estimated Rental Value of

PER £200 ANN.

The Property is held on lease direct from the Freeholder, for a
term of 95 years (from last Lady-Day)

An example of a key pattern
similar to that in the stucco
above the second floor
windows of Wyand's first
houses: Nos. 90–108
& 57–75.

A coal-hole cover in the pavement,
many of which remain as
reminders of the coal fires
burning in the stoves and
grates of every room when
these houses were occupied
by whole families. Some
were locally made at
ironworks in Notting Hill,
like this one outside the
basement entrance to No. 94.

In some Conservation Areas these have been regarded as of sufficient
interest to be preserved, but their numbers tend to dwindle. In August
1995 there were 125 still in place in the pavements. West of Marloes
Road there were 26 on the north and 22 on the south. Around the
northern side of the Garden there were 32, and to the south only 12.
The southern curve to Cromwell Road had 12 on the west side and 21
on the east.

About half of the iron lamp-posts have been replaced by concrete ones
probably as a result of war damage. One seems to be missing altogether
outside No. 81.

The Victorian pillar box on the
corner near No. 25 probably
looked like this. Rather sadly it
was replaced by a King George V
one by McDowall, Steven & Co.
Ltd of London and Glasgow. As
the king died in 1936, it cannot
have been installed during his
reign through bomb damage,
unless shortages led to an out-
dated box being put here in
1940–41.

BY ORDER OF MORTGAGEES.

For Occupation or Investment.

An Important Commodious Town Residence, very conveniently situate, in a high-class Residential District.

PARTICULARS AND CONDITIONS OF SALE

OF No.

87, Lexham Gardens

CROMWELL ROAD,

KENSINGTON,

CONTAINING :—

Ten Bed and Dressing Rooms, Two Bathrooms, Fine Double Drawing Room, Large Dining Room and Library, and Ample Domestic Offices.

MODERN DRAINS. ELECTRIC LIGHT

Pleasant Garden in Rear.

Held for about 63¼ years unexpired at £5 per ann. Ground Rent.

To be offered at the MART, Tokenhouse Yard, E.C., by Messrs.

CHESTERTON & SONS

ON

Thursday, 30th May, 1907,

At **TWO** o'clock.

Solicitors—
   Messrs. HEWLETT, BIRCH-REYNARDSON & BUCKNILL,
          2, Raymond Buildings, Gray's Inn, W.C.
Auctioneers—
   Messrs. CHESTERTON & SONS,

	Telephones:—
116, Kensington High Street, W. ;	{ Kensington 450
	{ Western 204
15, Sloane Street, S.W. ;	Kensington 16
52 & 53, Cheapside, E.C. ;	Bank 5466
and at Norbury, S.W.	Streatham 85

The cover of a Chesterton's sale brochure (1907)

5

The Earlier Background of the Lee Abbey Houses

The Early Inhabitants of Nos. 57–67

It is a curious fact that from the earliest days the needs of students were being served by some of those who lived in this section of the street. However, first let us consider the houses individually. There is an oddity about No.57 for it seems to have been linked to a Christian organisation since before it was built. The archives of the Young Women's Christian Association record that the lease of this property, 'Marloe House', was acquired, probably by gift, on the 29th September 1874. At this time there was only a building plot, and it was some years before it was ready for use. However, a dealer in works of art, Edward Fox White, was probably the first occupant of No.57 about 1879. He lived here with his wife and six children, and five servants until about 1890, when he moved next door, apparently still retaining possession of No.57 according to the rate books, when it was leased to Captain Walter James (see above, pages 26–30) and later to John Masters, M.D. (1895).

No.59 Seems to have been first occupied by James Anderson, a retired manufacturer who also had six children. He owned the house for about ten years. In 1891 it was occupied by a widow of private means with four children and seven servants to run the home. Very soon Fox White took it on, and moved in. He was followed by A. de B. Phillips, of whom later.

Edward Walker, F.R.S. was the first to live at No.61, but in about 1881 another merchant, William Hughes Daunt, arrived. He was already in his fifties and probably stayed until his death fifteen or more years later.

Moving westwards, No. 63 seems to have had the longest connection with young people and students. From the first leaseholder, J. D. Hackney, whose wife was a schoolmistress, there were young people in education here. By 1881 Mrs Hackney had been widowed and was herself 70 years of age. She kept seven servants including a Housekeeper and a sick nurse. There was also a teacher of French and German in the house but by now there was only one pupil, a girl of seventeen (although the Census may have been taken during a holiday period). By about 1885 Miss Eliza G. Woods, another schoolmistress, was here obviously running a finishing school for young ladies. At the Census of 1891 she had a house full of eleven adults, including teachers and servants and an equal number of girl pupils aged between 15 and 18. Of these two were from Ireland, two from Wales, two from Scotland, two from Cumberland (probably sisters), one from Lancashire, one from Cheshire, and one from Essex, which represented a very good spread from around Great Britain. After some years Miss Woods was followed by Miss Crease.

W. N. Duckworth was the first at No.65, soon followed by Leveson Edward Scarth, a young Oxford man of independent means now studying medicine. Around 1885, Henry Howard, a career diplomat moved in from No. 85 and kept this as his London base for the next dozen or more years. In 1891 he was away, probably serving abroad, but the house was occupied by his wife, daughter and their servants. He was already a Companion of the Bath, and rose to be quite a distinguished ambassador with a knighthood, finally serving with the British Mission to the Pope. Charles Peile, a practising barrister, took a fourteen year lease on No.67 in 1879. The house was later the retirement home of the Reverend W. H. Milman. His father had been Professor of Poetry at Oxford, while Vicar of St Mary's Reading; the author of the hymn, 'Ride on! Ride on in majesty!', he was later a distinguished Dean of St Paul's. The son wrote his father's *Life*, but did not achieve the same prominence.

So much for early residents. Let us move on to the surprisingly long history of providing residential accommodation on this site, and those who were responsible for the first beginnings of turning these houses from family homes into wider uses.

From Casa Quinta to Suncourt Hotel

Arthur de Beauvoir Phillips had lived at No.59 for several years, as we have seen. Presumably he died in 1909 for Mrs Phillips is then listed at both Nos.59 and 61. Perhaps she thought to run a boarding house in them together. Anyway, in 1910 two important changes occurred in the houses which have developed into Lee Abbey. About the same time Number 57 began to be run as a hostel by the Young Women's Christian Association (YWCA). This organisation was concerned about the plight of single young women coming to London and the need to provide them with a secure place in which to live in this impersonal city, where they could be subjected to temptations and to the pressures which might not be helpful to them.

About the same time James Fiddes-Brown took over Nos.59 and 61 as a boarding house, and in the following year he added 63 to make what he then named the Hotel Casa Quinta. This private hotel, as it was described in the following year, was of course a very different proposition from a hostel. Fiddes-Brown was running this for profit.

Hotels in this part of London were few at this time, and I like to think of officers returning to the front in France during the First World War getting a little last respite from their leave, and Kensington did not suffer any air attacks in this war. Soon after that War ended in 1919 the enterprise was renamed the Lexham Court Hotel, still under the same proprietor. A few years later it became the Suncourt Hotel, presumably with a change of ownership, and it is interesting to note that planning permission was granted in November 1927 to join together numbers 59, 61, and 63 into one building (the houses in which today we have our Reception, Front Lounge and Dining Room. Some of the major internal changes no doubt date from this time.) Presumably these changes coincided with the change of ownership and name. Thirty years later (1957) the Suncourt Hotel was still occupying the same premises, having survived the Second World War, but not with out the threat of destruction and some very 'close shaves'.

1940: War Comes to Lexham Gardens

War came to this quiet residential street in September 1940. This time there was aerial attack, and Lexham Gardens was not unaffected. On the 7th both ends of the street were hit by high explosive bombs. Those at the back of the Arlington Hotel (Nos.1–3) caused casualties. A few minutes earlier the top of No.79 had been set on fire, and the top two floors of No.83 badly damaged. Three days later, the 10th, the Suncourt Hotel had a narrow escape when a high explosive bomb fell in the garden of No.65 leaving a crater 15 feet across and 12 feet deep (near to our present ornamental pond and fountain). Sufficient damage was inflicted on our buildings that those living in the YWCA hostel at No.57 had to be re-housed in a hotel. This house was then used as a store and did not re-open as a hostel until 1944. On the 12th a high explosive device fell into the parish church of St Philip, causing considerable damage and the destruction of stained glass windows, including the great east window. On the 13th, No.101 was set on fire, and on the 26th a bomb fell in Earl's Court Road opposite No.146.

October had fewer incidents, but on the 7th No.51 was very badly damaged leaving ten casualties and two dead. Something of the difficulty of rescue work is shown by the fact that one body was found at 8.30.a.m. and it was thought that there was only one dead. The second body was not discovered in the rubble until 1.30.p.m. St Mary Abbots Hospital suffered some damage in the raid but no casualties. This hospital developed around the old work-house, a beautiful building occupying large grounds immediately behind the north side of Lexham Gardens east of Marloes Road, now being re-developed as Kensington Green. On the 15th the Suncourt was set on fire at the front and the back by incendiaries. The damage in November began when Nos.180–194 Cromwell Road were hit by three high explosive bombs very early in the morning of the 9th. This is the row of houses behind Lee Abbey including the site on which the Sherborne Court flats have since been built. The Hospital behind Lexham Gardens received a direct hit on the 14th. 'C' Block was put out of action and four people were killed. Nos.64–70 Lexham Gardens were damaged on the early evening of the same day by two high explosive bombs, and both Nos.64 and 66 partly collapsed. Then in the early hours of the 15th another high explosive bomb damaged Nos.45 & 49, partly demolishing No.47.

Mercifully there were no casualties in November. Remember that there will have been frequent air raid warnings throughout these many months, during which people took shelter wherever possible. In another part of London I can remember often being put to bed for the night in an underground shelter in the garden, with the never-to-be-forgotten drone of the engines of the enemy bombers, the sound of exploding shells and the whine of falling bombs before the ground shook with the detonations.

In December only one incendiary device fell on Lexham Gardens and caused no damage. The worst of the blitz was over, but on 11th May 1941 another high explosive bomb in the vicinity of No.51, which was already being demolished after the severe damage in the previous September, caused further damage. The long term result was that Nos.45–53 were replaced altogether by the new development of Lexham House. St Mary Abbots Hospital was hit for the third time in the early hours of the same day. Fortunately there were no casualties and the medical work did not suffer and mercifully the 11th May 1941 proved to be the last night of the 'blitz'. A local resident, Vere Hodgson, wrote on that Sunday: 'Just trying to recover from last night! We had a terrible time, but mercifully are still intact. The wailers went at 11.p.m ... what a night. Bombs came down in dozens.'

Three years later Hitler was able to renew his attacks on London. In February 1944 a bomb near No.86 caused neither casualties nor damage there, but four people were killed in the hospital behind. Still worse was yet to come, with the Flying Bomb and the V.2 rocket. Early on the morning of the 17th June the first PAC (Pilotless Air Craft) fell on Kensington. It scored a direct hit on the nurses' home and a children's ward at St Mary Abbots Hospital. First reports were of 2 dead, about 30 injured and 15 people trapped. The final death toll was eighteen - five nurses, six children and seven adult patients. The same Kensington resident, who saw the damage next day wrote:

> Went along Marloes Road ... great piles of glass marked the route. Heavy Rescue lorries were driving in and out and gathering up the debris. All one roof of the hospital gone.

Naturally there were effects on the wider locality. Much of the eastern section of Lexham Gardens suffered damage from the blast and of course the whole area would have been badly shaken. On the day after this attack Vere Hodgson wrote:

> These last three days have been one long Air Raid Alert, and we have had little sleep ... These Robot Planes go on after daybreak, which the old raids never did.

What were originally called pilotless aircraft were soon renamed 'Flying Bombs' because that sounded less terrifying. However they were a fearsome weapon of war. Again I have many memories of the rough noise of the engines, the terror when they ceased, and the unpredictability of their course. Sometimes the engines cut-out and the machine nose-dived, sometimes they glided on silently for miles. Living on the very edge of unspoilt rural Surrey and yet within the borough of Croydon, our wartime home was right in one of the flight path corridors along which V1s came. I had every reason to be expert in their sounds for more Flying Bombs (141) fell on Croydon than on any other London borough, mainly between the middle of June and the end of August 1944. Kensington and Chelsea escaped with only 20, but not without the tragic hit on St Mary Abbots Hospital, and direct hits at the junction of Earl's Court Road and Kensington High Street, full of shoppers, and another in Kensington Church Street, causing much damage and loss of life.

Her Majesty the Queen (now the Queen Mother) observed after the bombing of the Guards Chapel, near Buckingham Palace, full of worshippers on a Sunday morning, and a day after the attack on the hospital: 'there is something very inhuman about death-dealing missiles being launched in such an indiscriminate manner.' Flying Bombs were in fact among the last vile acts of an evil and despicable regime which was also responsible in its last dying months for the worst excesses of the death camps. It is wrong ever to forget the depths of cruelty to which human beings can descend.

Peace is Restored

Lexham Gardens escaped the V.2 rockets, and then at last residents here in Kensington will have joined in the great celebrations, which we have been recalling this year (1995) in London, marking the end of such threats of terror and sudden death which came with VE (Victory in Europe) Day, 8th May 1945, and later that year the return of a lasting peace.

After the War life continued amid shortages. In 1951 came the Festival of Britain, soon followed by the death of King George VI who had done so much in his quiet way to be identified with the suffering of Londoners in war, staying in Buckingham Palace and indeed being bombed there. With the coronation of his daughter in 1953 Britain really seemed to have shaken off the drabness and austerity of the war, and prosperity began to return also.

This part of Kensington also began slowly to look up again after a period of declining fortunes. It is interesting to note that when 'the well converted property' No.67 was offered for sale freehold by Knight & Co., Auctioneers, in January 1952, it was with the caution that 'certain War Damage repairs remain to be carried out to the property' even though it had not suffered a direct hit.

By 1958 the Suncourt had added No. 65 (our ground floor with the Chapel, Study Room, and secretaries). By 1967 the last two houses were acquired, No.67 (the Warden's Flat) and the hostel at No.57 (thus making the opening up of the Garden Lounge possible). The Suncourt was owned by M. F. North, Ltd (North Hotels Ltd). It is interesting to note that they purchased No.57 from the YWCA at the end of 1967, apparently for the astonishingly low price of £1,500, only half of what it would have cost when new ninety years earlier. The owners obtained plans from Mountford, Pigott and Partners for extensive alterations when incorporating the two additional properties into the unity of the existing four. This hotel expansion reflects the boom in this area which accompanied the existence of the West London Air Terminal of British European Airways. From the late 1950s this occupied the site of the present Sainsburys Supermarket in Cromwell Road, near to Gloucester Road Underground. The line to Heathrow had not yet been built, and in those days travellers gathered in Kensington before being bussed out to the airport there. This terminal closed at the end of 1973, and shortly afterwards B. E. A. joined up with others to become British Airways.

Nos. 57–67, which became united as a hotel between 1910–67, and were later altered by the Lee Abbey Community.

6

Lee Abbey in London:
Courtfield Gardens

The Devonshire Inspiration

Meanwhile another development had been taking place in the immediate vicinity of the terminal, just across Cromwell Road in Courtfield Gardens. We must go back to the Second World War, and distant Devonshire, to understand why.

The Reverend Roger de Pemberton was a charismatic figure. In the years before the Second World War he had run house parties for young people in various locations. War brought these to an end, but within a year or two they were resumed and in August 1943, and again in 1944, one was located at a large country house called Lee Abbey.

Murray's guide book of 1872 somewhat scathingly asserts that 'Lee was never the site of any monastic foundation. It is only a melodramatic abbey.' Nevertheless the Lee Abbey estate near Lynton, on the edge of Exmoor in North Devon, had been part of a manor gifted to the Cistercian Abbey of Forde in Dorset about 1200 by Henry de Tracy, though it had first come to the King after the Norman Conquest. At the Reformation it became Crown land again in 1539. By the end of that century it was in private hands, and became the base of a family now powerful in the locality. *Lorna Doone* by R. D. Blackmore was published in 1886. John Ridd, the hero living two

centuries earlier near Oare a few miles away from Lynton,
refers to 'De Wichelhalse, our great magistrate ... at Ley
Manor.' Here he describes a visit:

> When we arrived ... we were shown very civilly into the
> hall, and refreshed with good ale and collared head, and the
> back of a Christmas pudding. I had never been under so
> fine a roof (unless it were of a church) before; and it
> pleased me greatly to be so kindly entreated by high-born
> folk.

Of course Blackmore's book is an historical novel, but it
includes the happy fact that John Ridd renewed his court-
ing of Lorna in a nobleman's house in 'the village of
Kensington', and there the incident occurred which won
him his knighthood, shortly before a new King acquired
Kensington Palace (see page 5). In reality the Wichelhalse
family had enlarged a gabled farmhouse into a manor
'when the coming of plague to Barnstaple drove them from
the town into the safer countryside' in 1628. Sadly they did
not find a refuge at Ley (or Lee as we know it) for much
more than a generation or so. As Murray tells the story:

> Here, in former times, stood the splendid abode of the De
> Wichelhalse, a noble family of Holland, who, about 1570,
> during the persecution of the Protestants by Alva, escaped
> with their property to England. In the reign of Charles II,
> Sir Edward De Wichelhalse was the head of this house, and
> an important personage; but his daughter, his only child,
> proved the unfortunate cause of destruction to the family.
> She was wooed and won by a nobleman in high favour
> with James II; the lover proved faithless, and the deserted
> maiden was one day found lifeless under the rocks of Duty
> Point. The father in vain petitioned the king, and when
> Monmouth landed at Lyme, De Wichelhalse and his
> adherents hastened to support him. After the battle of
> Sedgemoor [at which the Duke of Monmouth, claimant to
> the throne of James II, was defeated and later executed] the
> unhappy parent returned to Lynton, but the emissaries of

the king were soon despatched to apprehend him, and, on their approach by the neighbouring valley, De Wichelhalse and the remainder of his family embarked in a boat to escape. The night was, however, stormy, and they are supposed to have all perished, as they were never heard of again.

All this was in 1685, but the 'Story of Jennifred', the daughter, which is 'associated in the minds of all visitors with Duty Point' is no more than wonderful romantic nonsense put about by an early Victorian clergyman in Lynton, Matthew Mundy. Years later this was shown up as a fabrication resulting from 'his insufficient knowledge of the Wichelhalses' by a Vicar of nearby Parracombe who wrote a careful history. The family was in fact an old Devonshire one, and there never was a Sir Edward with a daughter dead upon the rocks below the cliffs in such circumstances. Indeed the Squire Wichelhalse of the day was an active royalist, persecuting the defeated rebels. The true story is also a tragedy. The family had lost the estate in 1713, and Mary Wichelhalse, the last of that name, insisted on returning. She came up to the old house and 'wandered about by the cliffs gazing on the lost inheritance of her race ... and according to one account fell off the cliffs at Ley, or by another was washed off the rocks by the tide, the body never being found.' (See Plate 10a).

By the mid nineteenth century the old manor house had fallen into decay, and in 1841 the estate was bought by Charles Bailey. The new squire soon re-built the house as Lee Abbey and his son, C. F. Bailey, lived there until his death in 1919 when the estate was sold and became a luxury hotel. During the Second World War a preparatory school called Brambletye, from East Grinstead in Sussex, was evacuated there. de Pemberton hired the building during the school summer holidays.

Anticipating that Lee Abbey would be sold when the Prep School was able to return to Sussex at the end of the

War, he resolved to buy it as a permanent site for an expanded Christian centre. The purchase price was £28,000 and finance was a problem. Only after the commitment had been made to buy the estate did de Pemberton hear of a £6,000 legacy which he then loaned as the down payment for a mortgage. The house had become very dilapidated since the days of the luxury hotel, but with much self help Lee Abbey opened in June 1946 as a permanent centre run by a community of Christians with de Pemberton as the first Warden. (See Plate 10b).

Over the following years the work developed and prospered. It is also pleasing to note the comments in Pevsner's *Buildings of England: Devon* that 'the mansion, in sumptuous ham-fisted Gothic ... c.1850 ... .incorporating an older manor house of the Wichelhalse family' has been 'sensitively adapted and extended as a conference and residential centre for the Lee Abbey Fellowship', though the red-tiled roof is rather startling. From among the many who stayed there on holiday or on retreat there grew the 'Friends of Lee Abbey' who supported the work by their prayers and by other practical means. The Lee Abbey property is in the hands of Trustees and the movement is directed by a Council. In 1953 the chairman was Bishop Cuthbert Bardsley of Croydon. At the annual Council conference in January of that year various ways of developing the work of Lee Abbey were discussed. One idea was that there should be a 'London house'. There were some good reasons for this suggestion, but also some real reservations. Nothing developed along these lines, but ten years later Lee Abbey, London, came into being in very different circumstances. Yet the seeds were already being sown which led to this new development in Kensington.

Mrs Louise Locke first visited Lee Abbey in 1949. She was in poor health, unhappily married and had recently moved into a house in South London which was much too large for her. As a result of her visit she came to Christian faith and returned the following year with her children. There had been no response to her advertising for lodgers in London until she received a telephone call from Miss Hilda Porter of Methodist International House asking her to take overseas students. Mrs Locke had no experience of such students herself but was persuaded. The first to arrive was Pushpa, a young Indian from Singapore, who had come to London to study law. Over the next eight years Mrs Locke not only accommodated overseas students herself but she encouraged others, including Lee Abbey Friends, to do the same.

Two men were also particularly instrumental in foment-ing ideas which led to Lee Abbey, London. Lieut.-Colonel George Grimshaw was Secretary of the Overseas Visitors Department of the Church Missionary Society in London. I have my own memories of the concern among Christians in the late 1950s and early 1960s about the flood of over-seas students coming to Britain and the lack of facilities for them. On coming down from Cambridge in 1959 I followed up a suggestion from my College Chaplain to find out what was being done in London for the 25,000 such students. I visited a number of the more obvious Christian organisations.

The two individuals who stand out in my mind were Freddie Crittenden of the Inter-Varsity Fellowship, who had earlier been tutor to the young Kabaka of Buganda, and George Grimshaw of C. M. S. George was formulating his ideas for a Christian Institute. He was convinced of the need for club facilities, with a nucleus of students and a resident Christian community. Working and praying together the community would establish a centre which would provide a meeting place where seminars and intro-ductions could be made, at what he called a 'Christian intelligence centre'. Thus by 1960 there were ideas around which eventually led to the establishment of Lee Abbey London. Little did I realise when I met George Grimshaw that two years later I would be welcoming overseas students at the railway station in Leeds, and sharing my flat with a Nigerian medical student. I could not know when I met Freddie Crittenden that a few years later I would follow him in working in Uganda. Most surprisingly of all, perhaps, is the fact that thirty five years after that College Chaplain had sent me around London, Simon Barrington-Ward would have become Bishop of Coventry and Chairman of the Lee Abbey Council.

The catalyst in bringing together the ideas which led to Lee Abbey in London was Jack Winslow, Chaplain at Lee Abbey, Devon. From Eton and Balliol he had been ordained into the Church of England and had gone to India with the Society for the Propagation of the Gospel. After his first leave he had returned and founded an ashram, a small community in which Indians and Europeans lived a simple common life. They dressed and ate as Indians, but within a Christian community. Many years later he came to Lee Abbey in 1948 at the age of 65, having just retired as Chaplain at Bryanston School in Dorset. He therefore had much experience of various kinds of community when, about 1960, he read a life of St Francis. He was greatly impressed by the 'Chapter of Mats' held at Assisi in March 1221. This was a meeting at which the future of the Franciscans was debated by the 5,000 who attended this impressive gathering. The curious name came from the great many small huts built around Porziuncula to accommodate them. They were covered in woven willow branches and rushes, so that as the inhabitants of Assisi looked down on them from the city walls above it looked as though the Franciscans were sheltered by mats.

Winslow saw the need for a 'Chapter of Friends' to do something similar for the Lee Abbey movement. It was a large task to organise it – though this time bringing together only five hundred of such Friends for a week in September 1961. The Revd Gordon Mayo, one of the Lee

Abbey Chaplains, was responsible for administration and for accommodation in the guest houses and hotels in the vicinity. So there were no 'mats', but daily meetings were held in a large marquee on the north lawn at Lee Abbey, under the title, 'Task for Tomorrow'. Out of this week, seven serious suggestions emerged, which were later discussed by the Council. Most of these did not develop, but continued concern for overseas students was considered by a fact-finding committee which included George Grimshaw and Louise Locke; it was chaired by Gordon Mayo.

1961 was to be an auspicious year, with the British Government being prepared to make up to three million pounds available to voluntary bodies for capital expenditure via the British Council. This was to be geared to projects involving Commonwealth young people, and interest free loans would be available through the Overseas Students Welfare Extension Programme, and written off over twenty five years. The London County Council also offered loans.

The Committee was now chaired by Denis Wakeling (afterwards Bishop of Southwell and Chairman of the Lee Abbey Council). Through Lee Abbey Friends, attention was drawn to some hotels which were for sale in Courtfield Gardens and George Grimshaw went to look at them. Three separate buildings had been run as one by the Overseas Visitors' Club which provided for Australians and white South Africans who came to stay in London. In 1961 South Africa had left the Commonwealth and the Club closed. The three hotels, Little Britain (26–27 Courtfield Gardens), Edinburgh Court (56–57 Courtfield Gardens), and Melbourne Court (26–27 Collingham Road) were to be auctioned separately on the same day. As the auction proceeded Lee Abbey successfully purchased the first, Edinburgh. Then Melbourne was put up for sale, and went to a higher bidder above the agreed limit. There was no point in even bidding for the third, which happily was withdrawn. However, within twenty-four hours the new owner of Melbourne was willing to let Lee Abbey have it for the price paid, and Little Britain (later called Courtfield) was bought as well. Together they cost £236,000; only £6,000 had to be found immediately by Lee Abbey and many saw this purchase as miraculous.

What of the Community?

Gordon and Sheila Mayo were the obvious couple to run it, with their considerable experience in Kenya and in Devon. Three other key people also came from Devon: Lily Dear, the Secretary, Mary Hopper, the Head Cook, and Chris Mail, the House leader. These five moved into Melbourne in January 1964. Soon the Community had grown to twenty one, and they were serving 180 students: one hundred from Commonwealth countries, thirty from elsewhere abroad, and fifty from Britain. By October 1964 these places had been filled with students from thirty-nine countries and six different religions, with about two-thirds Christians. The British Council grant was dependent upon not proselytising, which was never the Lee Abbey intention. The vision was for a Christian presence at the heart of the Club, rather than simply seeking to make converts. The belief was in God's calling to the Community to witness in three major areas: 'their work, their life and worship, and their words.' This is still true today. In work the task was 'the provision of good quality hostel accommodation. This was easier said than done.' We know how true that still is! At first 'the Club offered some of the best-appointed student accommodation in London, but as the years went by it gradually became worn and shabby ...' In running somewhere like Lee Abbey, London, the challenge is far from simply to provide the capital outlay to set it up, but the ongoing need to maintain adequate standards is perhaps a greater test.

Life and worship within the Community have always embraced a wide ecumenical spectrum of Christian practice. It is important, however, never to lose sight of the fact that Lee Abbey is firmly within the Church of England tradition.

Anglican devotion should never be exclusive of other forms, but the particular Anglican emphasis on liturgy and sacrament should be clearly maintained. This was tellingly demonstrated by Gordon and Sheila Mayo who adopted a small anchor cross as the lapel badge of the Community. Though it was an ancient Egyptian symbol in origin, it also expressed a significance expounded by one of the Seventeenth century Anglican metaphysical poets, John Donne, Dean of St Paul's in his address to another of them, George Herbert. Of course Herbert wrote the hymn which includes these two verses:

> Teach me my God and King,
> in all things Thee to see;
> And what I do in anything,
> To do it as for Thee.
>
> A servant with this clause
> Makes drudgery divine;
> Who sweeps a room, as for Thy laws,
> Makes that and th'action fine.

This seems to me perfectly to express the calling of the Lee Abbey Community to serve God and our fellow human beings in every day things. Not long before his death Donne had gifts engraved on stone and set in gold, with the figure of Christ crucified engraved on an anchor (the emblem of Hope) rather than on a cross, sent in affection to some friends. One of these he also addressed in a poem in Latin: 'To Mr George Herbert, with one of my Seals, of the Anchor and Christ.'

The Crosse (my seal at Baptism)
   spred below,
Does, by that form, into an Anchor
   grow.
Crosses grow Anchors; Bear, as thou
   shouldst do
Thy Crosse, and that Crosse grows
   an Anchor too.
But he that makes our Crosses
   Anchors thus,
Is Christ, who there is crucified for
   us.

Thus Donne speaks of the Christian life. It is outwardly symbolised by baptism at which the sign of the cross is marked in water upon the forehead of the believer. This outward act is empty without the inner reality of a life in which Christ is central. Such a life is anchored in that sure foundation, which is how Jesus spoke of the reality of faith in himself. This cross, therefore, developed into the shape of an anchor, truly demonstrates the fact that the Christian life is wholly dependent upon Jesus, who not only died upon the cross for us, but is the daily 'author and finisher of our faith.' When Herbert died, his seal was found wrapped in some verses which included these lines:

When winds and waves rise highest, I am sure,
This Anchor keeps my faith, that, me secure.

The Official Opening – November 1964

It was some months before the formal opening occurred. This was a notable occasion with many visitors sharing in it, and in particular the Mayor of Kensington, Councillor Mrs John Walford, and Bishop Bardsley now of Coventry (Chairman of the Lee Abbey Council). The ceremony was carried out by the Right Honourable the Earl of Wemyss and March, a notable Scottish Christian, now much involved in student concerns, who had worked in Africa, and was also Chairman of the National Trust for Scotland. In his address he said, 'Without sounding too gloomy a note I believe Christians have a particularly big job in this country in preventing the racial situation becoming much worse than it is. This situation makes it difficult for students from overseas to find suitable accommodation.' The Overseas Visitors' Club had been known as 'Little Britain' and he went on to say that 'It seems highly significant that it did not survive.' In her speech the Mayor said, that 'young people coming to London for the first time could feel terribly lost and lonely ... This is providing a real home where they can feel wanted, and to feel wanted is one of the most important things to every one of us in this life.'

What of the Students?

Those who stayed for any length of time soon came to be known as 'Residents'. We have seen the rough composition of the initial intake as it was in October 1964, with the great emphasis on those from Commonwealth countries, and in practice with a majority from a Christian background. It is also interesting to note that their costs for a single room were £5. 15 shillings (£5.75) per week, and sharing a triple room only £4. 10 shillings (£4.50). Changing conditions have brought a different composition of people, and higher charges! Sadly, in many ways, the Commonwealth connection has lessened as economic realities made further education in London more expensive. Numbers from African countries dropped, while the proportion from Asian and Middle Eastern countries increased. It is simplistic to suppose that this shift in geographical location necessarily meant any significant change in religious backgrounds. There are many Christian students from Asian and Middle Eastern countries, as well as many Hindus or Muslims; it is dangerous to make naive assumptions. However, it is true to say that over the past thirty years students have increasingly come from wealthier countries or more affluent circumstances. This needs to be borne in mind especially perhaps in considering what material standards are required to meet our claim to provide a 'home from home'.

Changing needs were also demonstrated in the purchase of a fourth property in the Courtfield Gardens area in 1968. This was Sedan House, at 12, Collingham Road, and it was acquired to provide bed sit accommodation for married couples. The demands of running the London house of Lee Abbey were only increased by such provision.

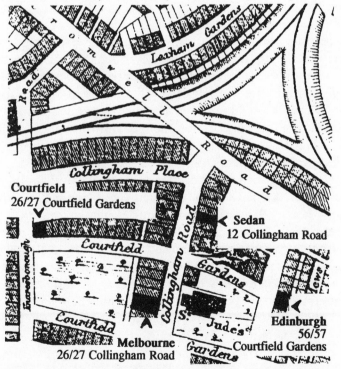

Courtfield Gardens, (See Plate 11)
showing the scattered Lee Abbey buildings 1964–1982.

7

The Move to Lexham Gardens

Coming Under One Roof

The trouble with Courtfield Gardens was twofold. Firstly
the buildings were ageing and needed a lot of attention.
Increasingly it was clear that there were problems with
having separate buildings. Surely it would be much simpler
to be under one roof? By 1980, after more than fifteen
years within the complexities of Courtfield, Edinburgh,
Melbourne, and then Sedan, such considerations had
become pressing reasons for change. But there were others
too. The basic needs of overseas students for a home in
London, rather than simply a place to reside in, remained
the same as ever. However, the clientele were changing, as
we have seen. It was easy for men like George Grimshaw
and Jack Winslow to think of providing for
Commonwealth students. It was also easy to support a
charitable foundation committed to providing a home for
those from less privileged backgrounds overseas, who were
grasping at the benefits of higher education and who were
desperately needed to return home to put their skills to use
and their qualifications to improve the lot of others. By
1980 it was equally easy to think that there was no such
incentive to provide for those who had no long standing
link with Britain or for those who themselves came from
privileged backgrounds of affluence. There were those

within the Lee Abbey movement who, for good reasons, believed that the day of Lee Abbey in London, and in its existing form, was over.

I recall facing similar comments when I returned from working in education in Uganda. There the need was obvious, in a country far from providing universal education. All secondary education was a privilege, and none of it was free. When I was pressed into taking up a Chaplaincy in an independent boarding school in Scotland there were those who pleaded the superior needs among less advantaged young people. The truth is, however, that Christians are called to work among people of every background, simply because all human beings have some needs which cut across all barriers of race, or class, or economics.

So it was that Lee Abbey commitment to provide a 'home from home' in London was reaffirmed. The task was now to search for a more suitable building in which to carry the work forward. That part of Kensington, between Earl's Court and Kensington High Street, had very clear advantages. It was, and is, a fairly cosmopolitan area, very centrally located for many places of further education. The streets are safe, communications are excellent (including those with international airports), and it is very easily accessible to the parks and places of interest. At this time there were a number of hotels for sale, due to the recent closure of the Air terminal at Gloucester Road, and the reduced demand for such facilities. It was not difficult therefore to consider possible alternatives.

After much looking around, the choice fell upon the Suncourt Hotel which, as we have seen, had grown over more than half a century into occupying the six houses numbered 57–67 Lexham Gardens. The accommodation was already geared to hotel uses. The houses had been connected internally. The number of people who could be accommodated overall was not appreciably less than at Courtfield Gardens. Moreover there was the added attraction of the six gardens at the rear of the houses being united into one in a singular way. Again, somewhat miraculously, the various properties in Courtfield Gardens found a single buyer, and this facilitated the purchase of the Suncourt block. Assisting Lee Abbey in all this was Colin Molyneux, a surveyor well experienced in the difficulties of London sales. He still marvels that this deal went through so smoothly. The story of the act of re-location became a drama in itself however, told in *The Lee Abbey Story* (see page 106–107 and Plates 12 and 13).

A Second Opening

The move was made spectacularly in a single day, on the 6th September 1982, and those who had breakfasted in Courtfield Gardens had supper in the new premises. The official opening ceremony did not take place until the 9th April of the following year. This time it was performed by the Right Honourable Lord Belstead, Minister of State at the Foreign and Commonwealth Office, the member of the Government responsible for overseas students. During the ceremony candles were lit, each by a representative person: Lord Belstead, the Lee Abbey Council Chairman, the wife of the first London Warden, the Warden from Devon, the new Warden here in London, and representatives from the Management and Residents' Committees. The Lee Abbey Chairman, Bishop Wakeling, dedicated the building. In his address he re-stated the task by saying simply:

> If we don't provide acceptable accommodation no students will come and stay with us. And if this was just Overseas student accommodation without any opportunity for Christian work no one would join the Community. The Christian Community here will seek to preach the Gospel by the sincerity of its life, the quality of its service, and its readiness to answer for its faith when necessary.

The new premises certainly provided much more suitable accommodation than had been possible in four separate buildings, and for six years the work of the Club continued without major interruption. By 1988, however, it was evident that urgent work was needed on the roof, and the bold decision was taken to re-build the Fourth and Fifth floors at the same time, and so provide purpose-built accommodation on those two floors. Work began in the following year. There were unexpected problems which led to major difficulties over finance. There was the need to raise a large bank loan, despite the extraordinarily generous giving of half a million pounds by Lee Abbey Friends. In 1989 there had been the celebration of the Silver Jubilee of the Lee Abbey work in London, and a Thanksgiving Service for this redevelopment was held when the Council met here on 11th June 1990. It was a great relief to all when the scaffolding and the sheeting came down after a whole year of disruption.

About the same time a lot of work was done on developing the wonderful facility of the garden. This had been derelict in the hotel days, and had already been greatly improved. Now the fish pool and fountain were added, close to where the bomb had exploded in 1940. Another addition was the terrace. Rosalind Oi Lin Cheng had come to Lee Abbey in 1988. Like many others over the years, she was a law student from Singapore. Two years later she joined the Community, but soon suffered a recurrence of cancer which led to her tragically early death in hospital after being nursed here by the Community as long as possible. The terrace was built in her memory in 1991.

Five years later we still have a full house, with high demand for student accommodation. The site is still ideally suited to those who study at a wide variety of institutions, and is in a part of London where the neighbourhood is only being enhanced. The building itself retains a lot of character, making it well suited to development as a 'home from home', but there is ongoing need for re-furbishment and repair. This is inevitable in a property which is one hundred and twenty years old and which gets no respite, since we operate throughout the year without a close. The challenge to raise the necessary finance remains, though we take seriously the fact that the most ready source of money is from our own efficient trading. Applications for places on the Community are also high, and we are able to choose those whom we believe are most able to follow God's call to serve him here. However, it is more challenging to attract the necessary leaders in such a team.

All in all, Lee Abbey in London remains an exciting place to be, and there is unlikely to be a 'dull moment' – at least for those who run it!

8

The Work of Lee Abbey
in London

The Challenge

Finally a word should be said about the Lee Abbey International Students' Club today. (This is to give its full title, though those who live here invariably called it simply, Lee Abbey).

Despite a greatly changing world, the task remains essentially the same as it was in 1964: to provide accommodation and meals in a homely atmosphere of safety and toleration. This is for students, regardless of age, background, race, or creed. Some are here for a few weeks, others for three or four years. Some have had brothers or sisters here before them, and now there are even the children of former Residents. If beds are not filled by students, we offer them to anyone and this is particularly so during July, August, and September, which we call "the transit season", less so in December (Christmas) and in April (Easter).

The Lee Abbey movement was founded by members of the Church of England and it remains within that tradition. Though officially approved by that Church it receives no financial support from it. Each of its parts are non-profit making charities. Any income is ploughed back into the work. At the same time it is necessary for us to look for financial support from others. We owe an incalculable debt to Lee Abbey Friends, many of them not well off, who have supported our work so generously over many years. We also need to look for backing of this kind from further afield, if we are to maintain standards which justify our claim to provide a real home atmosphere. No doubt we owe even more to those who pray for us.

The Community

Despite the clear Anglican background the movement is also very ecumenical, and has always attracted those from other Christian traditions. This is evident in some of those who come and stay as student residents. It is even more evident in the Christian community of around forty people who actually run the London Club on a daily basis. For this Community there is a faith requirement. Members must be able to assent publicly to their Christian faith and commitment when they first come here. Most come to be contracted for a period of one year. Occasionally it is for a shorter period, but this only increases the instability of an always constantly changing work-force, since very few organisations try to run on such a rapid turn-over of staff. A few stay for longer, especially those who have some particular responsibility of leadership, for the Community is divided into five teams. The Warden is assisted by five members of the Management Team who are concerned with all the responsibilities of general administration, personnel, and finance. There are four Heads of Department over House, Kitchen, Maintenance, and Office teams. The Lee Abbey Council is in overall control of all aspects of the movement which now includes the Devon estate, the London Club, and much smaller household communities in Aston near Birmingham, Knowle West in Bristol and Walsall in Staffordshire. Each of these is in a rather deprived area and they assist the churches in their out-reach there. Each of the

Communities also has a Committee of outside supporters to assist in advising the Warden over the 'financial and business side of the work'. Here in London this also acts 'as a support group to the Warden, Community and Students.' One aspect of this last is to assist the Warden in managing a Bursary scheme which may be used to help students who run into financial difficulties during their time here.

At present the majority of Community in London come from places outside Britain. We have a strong contingent of South Africans from mixed racial backgrounds; West and East Africa are also represented here, and there are Egyptians too. A number come from Eastern European countries including the Czech Republic, Hungary, Poland, Russia, and Slovenia. In recent months, those from other parts of Europe have included Dutch, German, Italian, Spanish, Swedish, and Swiss. Japan, New Zealand, and the United States are also represented. It is usual to have between fifteen and twenty nationalities on the Community at any one time. The student residents come from an even wider spectrum of the world, often including as many as thirty nationalities, or even more, at any one time.

It is also worth pointing out that Community members are required to live here, and they receive many payments in kind: their food, accommodation, heating and lighting are all provided, together with a weekly allowance in cash. When the word 'Volunteer' is applied to them it causes misunderstandings. Many of the Community are young school leavers, or recent graduates, and it is well to remember that the whole 'package' of remuneration given to the youngest Community member is more than double the value of a British Government student grant for London.

The Nature of Community Life

In these rather sad days of fanatic sects it is important to stress that Lee Abbey is not a commune where silly decisions might be taken by a simple majority. Our Community Manual states that: 'The Warden is appointed by Council to have oversight and care of the Community and to manage its business ... [and] ... is responsible for what happens and does not happen at [Lee Abbey in London], and is in turn responsible to Council.' Within the simple rule of life for everyone here there is the promise to 'accept the authority of those God sets over you in Community.' This authority is represented by the Warden, who is usually ordained in the Anglican ministry and is licensed to work here by the Bishop of London. Secondly, Lee Abbey is not a sect but stands firmly within the Church of England, and the Council is chaired by a diocesan Bishop. Thirdly, we do everything we can to encourage members to keep in close contact with their families while they are here, even giving a number of free telephone calls to them. Many Community members also have their parents, or other members of their family to stay here and see them, and such accommodation is provided for them at a very greatly reduced charge.

In whichever area of the movement we are serving, it is essential to recognise that being on Community is a way of life, and much more than simply having a job with fixed working hours. Of course, we want people to live a balanced life, and this will include having adequate time to worship, to work, and to relax in leisure. This includes having a firm commitment to a church for worship on Sundays, which is why we have no service here in the Chapel on that day. However, membership of the Community will also require a willingness to join in all the wider aspects of our work, including the social programmes and evening activities, without regard to narrow definitions of working hours. Being on Community is not a normal job, but a Christian way of life, and must be accepted in that spirit.

All this, of course, brings its own challenges. Our

ecumenical approach also means that we have Roman
Catholic, Orthodox, Coptic, Anglican (of various traditions), Baptist, Methodist, Pentecostal, and Charismatic
Christians all living and working together, and also
worshipping daily in our Community prayers and weekly
Holy Communion. As a Community it is very important
that we hold on to the unity which we have in our
common commitment to the Lord Jesus Christ. At the
same time we need to respect the differences of emphasis
which our own tradition brings to an interdenominational,
and international environment. No one form of liturgy or
complete freedom in worship will be right, any more than
one kind of music, or one type of praying. We can all gain
by being enriched by the spirituality of others, and just as
we all need to go on growing, so we can all learn from
others. Nevertheless it is right that we should maintain
something of the Anglican background from which this
movement has developed and in which we are all privileged to share. Something of a balance is maintained by
having some kind of liturgy in our worship on three days
in a week and more extemporary forms of worship on the
other three.

What of Religious Faith?

In *The Lee Abbey Story*, Richard More wrote of early days
in Courtfield Gardens that:

> a real affinity was experienced between those who were
> believers. The great divide was not so much between the
> Christians and the rest, as between those who were people
> of faith, be it Christian, Hindu or Muslim, and those who
> had abandoned their original belief in their attempts to
> assert their identity or break away from their past.

This must be the attitude of religious toleration in which
Lee Abbey in London continues to exist. At the same time

he also observed that 'although anybody was welcome to join the community at prayers, it was always made clear that this was Christian worship.'

Here is an important principle which we are right to maintain. We are a Christian foundation and we welcome people of all faiths and of none, and we wish all to feel at home. The only practice of religious worship therefore is Christian worship in the Chapel, very rarely expanded into the Dining Room, or exceptionally in the Garden Lounge. This is always Christian and for the Community, although others are always welcome. Our hope is that thus no one will feel threatened and yet anyone will feel welcome.

What of Our Words Therefore?

Christian witness should be seen in the quality of our daily work and in our worship. If these glorify God, the opportunity will come when we can speak. People will be curious to know of our motivation and of our reasons for being on the Community. If our work and worship are right, God will do his own work in our midst.

A Ministry of Reconciliation

Finally let us remember the Reverend Jack Winslow. In 1921 this Old Etonian missionary shocked Europeans in India by founding the Ashram of the Christa Seva Sangha (The Society of the servants of Christ). Six years later a permanent site was found on the outskirts of Poona, and this soon included a student hostel which was among

> the most important of our undertakings ... There was a rush of applications....In a few days the hostel was full up, with a waiting list. They were a mixed lot - Christians, Hindus and Moslems ... arts students, and students of agriculture, engineering and law. But under the genial inspiration of ... the first Warden, they settled in happily together.

It all sounds rather like the beginnings in Courtfield Gardens nearly forty years later. Indeed it may not be too fanciful to say that Lee Abbey in London stems from a vision which began in the Indian city of Poona, well known to some of the first inhabitants of Lexham Gardens from their service days. Later Winslow was influential in establishing the Union of the churches of South India. Later still we have seen him in Devon. He was active in reconciliation until his death in 1974, aged over ninety. The Warden with whom he had worked in Devon for fifteen years wrote this: 'We must never forget that the conception of the Chapter of Friends was wholly Jack's. All that has come out of the Chapter and the founding of the Students' Club in London we owe, under God, to that initial inspiration.'

One of the great privileges of being on Community is that we have the opportunity to overcome the divisions and prejudices which so easily interfere with human relationships, not only within the Christian churches but even more outside of them. We can all engage in that greatest work of reconciliation, which is the basis of what Jesus came into the world to do – to reconcile ourselves and God, and each of us with one another. Therein lies the hope of mankind.

Lee Abbey, North Devon

Lee Abbey, London lies in the Parish of St Philip's, where they have adopted the Prayer of St Benedict for regular use. His prayer has a particular relevance to us here, since the Cistercians who owned the Lee Abbey lands in Devon during the Middle Ages were a reformist group of Benedictines.

The Prayer St Benedict (480–543.A.D.):

> Gracious and Holy Father,
> give us wisdom to perceive you,
> diligence to seek you,
> patience to wait for you,
> eyes to behold you,
> a heart to meditate on you,
> and a life to proclaim you,
> through the power of the Spirit
> of Jesus Christ our Lord.
> Amen.

A Prayer for those who work within the Lee Abbey Communities:

> (First name anyone known to you)
>
> Heavenly Father,
> we pray for those whom we have named before you.
> We thank you for them.
> You know their needs before we ask.
> Bless them,
> and equip them with your Holy Spirit,
> for the work which you have for them to do this day.
> Supply their needs,
> and keep them faithful together with us,
> in your service within the Lee Abbey movement;
> so may your name be glorified through our Lord Jesus.
> Amen.

Appendix

The Lexham Gardens Houses (Builders and External Details)

All the houses here were built in the conventional late-Italianate terrace style:

Nos. 120–146, built by John Sprake in 1872–75.
(see Plates 1a and 15a).
He was a builder of Kinnerton Street, Belgravia. In 1866-69 he had built the extension of Cromwell Road to link up Gloucester Road with Fenelon Road (now called West Cromwell Road) for Lord Kensington, Robert Gunter, and Henry Browne Alexander, landowners.

These houses have four storeys over a basement. The facades are of white brick with stucco dressings. They have bay windows up to the first floor, and Doric porticoes. There are balconies with stone balustrades at first floor level, and above the first floor bay window. The porticoes are set back from the pavement, with steps up to the front door, and small gardens by the pavement, in front of the basement window.

Sprake also built the three houses numbered 97–101 Earl's Court Road. Nos.99–101 were later joined together as Mulwarrie House, with entrance at the side. This pair were then re-numbered No.150 Lexham Gardens, but in reality are not part of it.

Nos. 90–104, built by Samuel Juler Wyand in 1874–75.
(see Plate 1b.)
These houses all have five full storeys over basements, with attics above. The facades are fully stuccoed. They are flat fronted apart from deep Doric porches, with contrastingly shallow balconies in front of three very elongated first floor windows, surmounted by pediments. The second floor windows each have key patterns in the stucco above them. The third and fourth floors are divided by a broad cornice, supported by modillions with dentils beneath. This seems to isolate the family rooms from those of the servants above. The balconies have ironwork.

Wyand lived at No.104 (similar to that on the front cover) for thirty years until soon after his wife's death in 1911, and died about the end of the First World War. He came from farming stock in Norfolk, though his father had built in London. In 1871, then aged only 37, he described himself as a 'retired builder'. Any such respite was short-lived for in the following year he was building in Marloes Road and then, of course, very extensively in Lexham Gardens. At the Census of 1881 he described himself as a builder employing 20 men. Unlike his father, he avoided bankruptcy, and his sons entered professions, one of them becoming a dentist.

Nos. 57–75, built by Wyand in 1875-77
(see Front cover, Plates 1b and 12a.)
These are identical to Nos.90–104. No.69 is the only one with the stucco from the first floor upward remaining unpainted, showing the original stone-like effect.

The double portico, uniting the entrances to Nos.59 and 61 was designed by Mountford, Pigott and Partners, of Cromwell Place, in 1967. It is an eye-sore which should be replaced by the restoration of the originals.

The stone balustrade above the fourth floor of Nos. 57–67 was added as part of the re-building of the Fourth and Fifth floors for Lee Abbey in 1989–90 (see illustration on page 65). It links these houses externally into a gentle and unobtrusive unity. It is a feature wholly in keeping with the houses on the south side of Lexham Gardens to the east of Marloes Road, and is at present seen to particular advantage at the detached No.55. These houses were built by G. E. Mineard, as we shall see shortly.

This addition introduces a Mineardian touch to these houses by Wyand. The suitability of the balustrade can be judged from the photograph in Plate 2d, and the porch is illustrated in the photograph of the Suncourt Hotel in its later days discussed in Chapter Five (see Plate 12a).

Nos. 77–87, built by Wyand in 1875–79
(see Plate 1c.)
These continue the line of the facade treatment already given to Nos.57–75 but with minor alterations. There is a bay window on the ground floor and a pediment only above the central window on the first floor, not over all three. However the plan is different, with much less depth to the ground floor.

Nos 89–105, built by Wyand in 1875–78
(see Plate 1d.)
These are of an entirely different design. They are faced in white brick with stuccoed dressings. They have bay windows right up to the first floor, and a slightly different treatment of the upper storey windows. They have four main storeys instead of five, without attics originally in all probability. The storey heights are lower than in Nos.57–87. There are balconies with stone balustrades above the first floor bays, like Sprake's opposite, but no balconies at first floor level. No.89 has a wider porch, and Nos.101–105 are larger, with wider frontages. They are also each built as free standing with a slight gap between each house. Only the general similarity of the Doric

porches and ironwork gives any unity to the whole of this side of the road.

The twenty five houses built by Wyand on this south side, over four or five years, probably show a conscious effort on his part to provide a varied choice of housing for potential buyers. All Wyand's houses have porticoes extending to the street, with steps leading up from there, and none has a small front garden which is sometimes found with other builders.

After a century of peaceful existence No.105 achieved sudden notoriety. For three weeks from the 7th April 1980 it was the headquarters of the Middle Eastern plotters who seized the Iranian Embassy, also taking hostages. It was from Flat No.3 that they set off each day to spy out the activity round Princes Gate where the building was situated. Then on the morning of Wednesday, 30th April they vacated the flat and took the Embassy at gun point. Six days later the S.A.S. dramatically ended the siege, and out of the six terrorists, five were killed.

Nos. 106–108, built by Wyand in 1877
(see Plate 2a.)
These seem to have had only the four storeys above basements – built without the top storey, but this has been added to No.106 (the house on the right of the photograph in the Plate). They have two windows rather than one large one on the ground floor, and the plans are slightly different.

We now move to the east side of Marloes Road which was still to be fully developed:

Nos.72–78, built by Wyand in 1877.
(see Plate 14c.)
They are similar to Nos.77–87 which he was building at the same time. These also have five storeys above the basement. They are different in being faced in white brick and stucco dressings rather than stucco all over.

Nos. 80–88, 48–78 and 40–44, built by Wyand in 1877–84. (see Plates 5b, 6 and 9.)

Here Wyand continued to use the style developed in Nos.89–105, with basement and four storeys, but all have triple windows in the upper levels, as at Nos.101–105. There is however a minor variation at Nos.80–88 where balustrades over the porticoes replace the ornamental rails between thick dies used in his earlier houses. The balustrade appears also above the first floor bay. All Wyand's houses of this type have egg and dart mouldings on the facings round the windows. No.66, which suffered bomb damage, has been re-built with lower storey levels and looks out of keeping. (See plate 5b.)

Nos. 31–55, built by George Edward Mineard in 1875–76. (see Plates 2c and d.)

Mineard is an interesting builder about whom we know a good deal through his friendship with Sir Henry Cole, the founding Director of the South Kensington museums. He was Canadian in origin, born at St John's, Newfoundland, but later living in Devon and in Islington. By this time he was in his mid thirties, a substantial builder employing one hundred people by 1881. In his last years Cole become obsessed with the dangers of sewer gas and he toured Kensington for a suitable house before first renting and then buying houses built by Mineard in Philbeach Gardens. It is interesting to note that Cole was greatly impressed by a system of ventilation invented by Mineard to prevent sewer gas dangers, and Cole encouraged him to patent this. Cole was also drawn to Philbeach Gardens because of the communal garden, over the planting out of which Mineard sought his advice. Together they established a 'Fifth of November Club' to provide an annual display of fireworks there. Cole also secured for Mineard the contract to over-haul the sanitary arrangement at Sandringham, one of the newer Royal residences. Mineard's houses were distinguished by the excellence of the plumbing arrangements. He worked extensively on the Edwardes estate and built one hundred houses in the decade of the 1870s, including the thirteen in Lexham Gardens.

These are built of gault brick and stucco dressings – four main storeys over the basements, and are rather like Wyand's houses opposite, which may have been based on these by Mineard. The facade treatment is 'more assured' here. There are bays up to the first floor, but no balconies. The roofs of the porticoes are set back from the pavement, like Sprake's. Some have small front gardens inside the railings.

Nos.45–53 were destroyed as a result of bomb damage in 1940–41. In 1952 designs were drawn up by the architect Edward D. Mills, which according to the notes on the *Survey of London* in the National Monument Record 'show a much more interesting block of flats matching the storey heights of Nos. 41 and 55' than those actually built in 1954–56 by Morrison, Rose and Partners. This uninspired red brick block of flats is known as Lexham House. (See Plate 5a).

Nos. 19–29 and 20–34, built by William Ashfold in 1875–76 (see Plates 2b, 4b and 5c.)
Little is known about Ashfold. His houses provide yet another type. They are tall and mostly five storeys over basements. They are also deep, especially at Nos.20–34 which back onto the railway. There are heavy Doric porticoes reaching out to the pavement, and bay windows up to the first floor. There are first floor balconies with stone balustrades, and again above the first floor bays. The elevations have profuse cement ornamentation, which is basically Italianate in design but 'hardly elegant'. There are stone balustrades at roof level for Nos. 19 and 21, and between the windows of the fourth floor in Nos. 20, 22, 32 and 34.

Nos. 36 and 38, built by William Douglas in 1882–84
(see Plate 4c.)

Douglas was of an older generation of builders and one of the biggest in South Kensington. He had emigrated from Scotland in his twenties and eventually became very wealthy, living in a house in Barnes but coming to his office in Kensington in his black and yellow carriage with horses especially chosen for the speed with which they could convey him. His wife had her own carriage. He seems to have been on the point of retiring at the time that he was active here, but the death of a son led him to continue in business with disastrous results. He went bankrupt in 1888 with liabilities of over £600,000.

His two houses are of five storeys over semi-basements. It has been said that they 'bring a touch of the size and grandeur of Queen's Gate' where Douglas had been particularly active earlier. There are bays right to the third floor, porticoes to the pavement, and balconies at first floor level. There, and at the roof there are stone balustrades.

Nos. 110–118, built by James Whitaker in 1876–77.
(see Plates 3a and 15a.)

Whitaker was a Hammersmith builder, active in Kensington. Ten years later he was declared bankrupt, but was soon free to resume building operations elsewhere and in 1893 he was described in the *Illustrated London: Progress and Commerce* as 'a high-class builder and decorator'. These houses were described as among those which he had 'erected and fitted up in the most sumptuous manner.' The scope of his business was said to include:

> sanitation and ventilation in all its aspects or systems, comprising all the latest improvements; electric lighting and electric and pneumatic bells, gas-fitting and plumbing of every description; the laying of parquet flooring in all designs, and the levelling, cleaning, and polishing of existing floors; tiling of every description, including hand-

painted work, mosaics, encaustic, & c; art decorations in all
special branches such as special designs for furniture ...
Upholstery work is also included in this firm's business.

He built this 'highly individual group of houses' which do
not relate either to Sprake's on the west or to Wyand's on
the east. This seems to indicate that Lord Kensington's
surveyor had minimal control over the elevations in this
area. All the main living rooms could be accommodated on
the ground floor because there was more ground at the back.

They have four storeys over basements, and are basically
classical with their stucco dressings. Still there are hints of
the uncertainty in style which was beginning to come in by
the mid 1870s. Porches here have round arches, and are
supported on piers with alternate bands of brickwork and
cement. Now the original effect only appears here in
No.110. At Nos.112-116, the central three, the pediments
at first floor level are now plastered over, which is not
pleasing. They also have a fifth floor added which makes
them look like the boarding houses they had become
before the Lexham Gardens Hotel. There are no balconies,
only roofs over small porticoes set back from the pavement, as with Sprake. No.118 also has a badly altered
portico and a flattened pediment at the first floor.

Nos. 1–7 and 2–10, built by Stevens and Colls in 1875–77.
(see Plates 3b, 15b, and page 30.)
George Stevens and George Colls were in partnership from
Notting Hill. A few years later they ran into difficulties and
Colls became bankrupt in 1881, a year after Stevens had
suffered a similar experience.

Here they began with two linked pairs, Nos.1 and 3 and
5 and 7. These were almost identical to the houses built on
the north side of Cromwell Road to the east of the
Marloes Road entrance between 1871–72, all of which
have since been demolished to make way for the Cromwell
Hospital and the Elizabetta Hotel.

There are banded columns to the porticoes, fluted here
in the upper part with Corinthian capitals, and guilloche
bands are used in the frieze of the portico on the first floor
window architraves, and as a continuous string at second
floor level. The facades are faced with brick and stucco.
The surviving door cases are identical with handsome four
panelled doors and embossed bands around the panels.
There are balconies with stone balustrades at first floor
level over bay windows on the ground.

In 1971 planning permission was given for the destruction of Nos. 5 and 7 to make way for a new Yugoslav
Embassy. This was designed by Hanna and Manwaring. In
a letter dated 11 January 1972 the architects stated that

> we have designed the new building in such a manner that
> the floor and roof heights are similar to the adjoining
> buildings and architecturally in complete sympathy with
> the surrounding area. The facing materials of the new
> building will be carefully chosen to ensure that this design
> requirement is met wherever possible.

Not everyone will share their optimism (see Plate 4d), and
of this group of houses by Stevens and Colls only Nos. 1
and 3, and 2–10 Lexham Gardens remain.

*Nos. 9–17 and 12–18, built by William Henry Willis in
1877–78.*
(see Plates 4a and 15b.)
Willis was a builder who 'drifted in and out of
Kensington'. He had some association with Mineard.

Basically he copied Ashfold's house fronts immediately
to the north, though his houses are smaller. Generally they
are only four, not five, storeys over basements. There are
minor differences in the stucco dressings on the brick
facades. There are false balconies set into the facade in line
with the first floor windows, and stone balustrades at the
roof level.

What happened at the back of the houses in Lexham Gardens could vary greatly, and still can. Additions of many kinds have been made from the earliest days of Sidney Woolf. His son wrote about his mother's responsibilities with No.101, after his father's early death:

> She was also saddled with a long lease of a very large house requiring seven or eight servants and an expenditure which she now could not possibly afford. My father must have been oddly careless about money, for at his own expense he had built a large wing on to the back of the house in Lexham Gardens, though he was the lessee, not the owner, of it. This was a fatal thing to do, for the house thus became much the largest in the street, and so it was extremely difficult to let ...

Note on the Original Name and Numbering

The numbering of houses in Lexham Road, as it was called until 1878, was very curious. The first ones to be occupied were on the north side and to the west of Marloes Road. Here the fourteen houses built by Sprake between 1872 and 1875 were numbered from 1 to 27 beginning from Earl's Court Road. The even numbers from 2 to 16 were given to the houses built by Wyand in 1874–75, starting on the same side from Marloes Road. Those opposite, which were begun by Wyand in 1875, were numbered 1–11 as building plots but from No.55 at the Marloes Road end when built. The *Post Office Directory* for 1878, prepared at the end of the previous year, provides a very strange picture. Besides houses already mentioned, there were some to the east of Marloes Road, all with odd numbers and on the south side. Finally there is a second house numbered 1 at the Cromwell Road end, the same building that bears that number to this day. Lexham Gardens is shown as a side turning to the south beside the house now numbered 55, but then No.53.

The Re-Numbering

This muddle was rationalised by a resolution of the Metropolitan Board of Works on the 1st March 1878. Houses on the west and south side were now to be numbered from 1 to 105 and on the east and north side from 2 to 146, commencing at the end nearest to Cromwell Road, with the whole thoroughfare called 'Lexham Gardens, W.' Thus Nos.1–27 on the north side became Nos.146–120, while Nos.2–16 became Nos. 90–104. On the south side the changes were less dramatic with all those in double figures increasing by two. The series running west from Marloes Road began with No.57 instead of No.55.

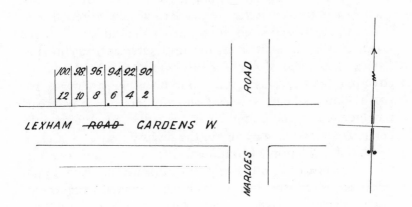

Acknowledgements and Sources

First of all I would like to express my warm thanks to those who have read this book in manuscript, made useful comments and given encouragement; these include Zoltan Aszalos, Boyd Auger, Douglas Evans, Simon Mason, April Pitman, Noel Walker, and members of my family.

I am most grateful to all those who have kindly given their consent for the use of copyright material used in the text. Any omissions in this respect are deeply regretted.

I have not discovered anything written about Lexham Gardens as such apart from the invaluable account in the *Survey of London*, Volume XLII, published in 1986, and covering South Kensington from Kensington Square to Earl's Court. That is necessarily limited, but my great indebtedness to the compilers of that splendid volume will be apparent, most especially in the discussions of the architecture. The National Monuments Record has the notes on this, but very little other relevant information. Additional information on the builder Whitaker comes from these notes (see pages 97–98), as well as the quotation on page 99.

There are quotations from the text of the *Survey of London*, Volume XLII as follows: page 13, about Logan is from p. 191 (and from *Kensington and Chelsea Street Names* (1980) p. 14); pages 13–14 about a second Belgravia: p. 403; page 14 about empty mansions: p. 400; pages 17–18: pp. 409–410; pages 39–40: p. 406. The map on page 10 is from figure 104: p. 240; the drawing on page 30 is adapted from figure 120: p. 296; that on the front cover is adapted from figure 119: p. 293 and reproduced in the Preface. All have been used with permission of the Royal Commission on the Historical Monuments of England (RCHME).

Boyd Auger points out that the cover illustration is incorrect since these houses were built with flat lead roofs (see page 48). Other Wyand houses do have pitched roofs (Plate 6a). He also sees an architect's hand in the well designed glazed screen bay facing onto the garden in Nos. 57–75 (see discussion on pages 39–40 and 98).

The Greater London Record Office preserves the papers of the Metropolitan Board of Works, and the District Surveyor's Records of the Middlesex Deeds Registry; until 1965 Kensington was part of that county. Details gleaned from such sources are minimal. That Office has the original of the map of 1812 reproduced on page 10, and the deposited copy of the Indenture from which the ground plan of No.57, owned by Lee Abbey, is taken (page 51); this also confirms that no architectural stipulations were made to the builder by the estate (see page 40). I am also grateful to the Local Studies Department at the main branch of the Royal Borough of Kensington and Chelsea Library in Hornton Street for the maps of 1867 and 1879 on page 18, and the Sale Brochure on page 56.

A number of general works about Kensington can be borrowed from the Public libraries. Among these is W. J. Loftie's *Kensington Picturesque and Historical* (1888), published by subscription, and 'By Command dedicated to Her Majesty The Queen' (Victoria). Thomas Tickell, Professor of Poetry at Oxford, published *Kensington Garden* in 1722 (see extract on page 19 which is the only part of descriptive relevance). Although the Local Studies department contains a great wealth of material about the locality, it is a matter of digging around if one wishes to pursue a particular study such as this. That department also has on microfilm copies of the Census records for 1881 and 1891.

These are only made available after one hundred years, but provide fascinating details of the inhabitants of the houses, though those away over night when the Census was taken were not recorded. Useful details can also be gleaned from the Valuation Lists (Rate Books) for the Parish of Kensington for the years 1886 and 1891.

The same department also has on microfilm copies of the local newspapers for Kensington, the *Post* and the *News*. Some of the details about 'Jimmy's', and about the opening of Lee Abbey in Courtfield Gardens are taken from these. Another valuable source of information about residents comes from the *Blue Guides*, and the *Post Office Directories* which are also in the Local Studies department, together with a most useful collection of local maps, all of which are well worth consulting. Estate Agents' sale brochures can also be found there; the earliest being for No.1 (1908), No.87 (1907), No.96 (1908), and No.110 (1909). There is also a wealth of information about casualties and bomb damage in the Second World War. The staff there are unfailingly helpful and enthusiastic.

One can read about William, second Lord Kensington in the *Creevey Papers* and in *The Napoleonists, a Study in Political Disaffection 1760–1960* by E. Tangye Lean (1970).

Essential details for other individuals are provided in the *Dictionary National Biography*, and *Who Was Who*, for relevant years. For some less prominent figures, Foster's *Men at the Bar* (1886), and the *Alumni Cantabrigiensis* and *Oxoniensis* are invaluable. Of the last two, the first is infinitely more useful because of the astonishing degree of detail which the second lacks, and because it covers matriculations up to 1900 rather than to 1886.

The extracts by Hermann Muthesius are taken from the English paperback edition (1987) of his book which was published as *The English House* in 1979, over seventy years after it was first published in Berlin as *Das Englische Haus* (1904–05). These are as follows: page 16: from p. 140; the first on page 42: p. 139, and the second and page 44: p. 140; pages 46-47: p. 141. Thanks are due for permission to Harper Collins *Publishers* Ltd and to Blackwell Science Ltd.

The Linley Sambourne House publications are also relevant, giving details of life in a house very similar to those in Lexham Gardens when they were first built. A visit there is strongly recommended on Wednesdays or on Sunday afternoons.

Captain James's letter from 5 Lexham Gardens to Lord Randolph Churchill about Winston quoted on pages 27–28 is in the Blenheim Papers and reproduced in *Winston S. Churchill*, Vol.1 (1966) by Randolph S. Churchill: pp. 190–191. The extract about 'Jimmy's', from pages 42–43 of Winston Churchill's own book, *My Early Life* (1930), on pages 28–29 is by kind permission of Macmillan General Books.

The passages in Chapter Three are from the paperback edition of the first volume of Leonard Woolf's autobiography: *Sowing: An Autobiography for the Years 1880–1904* (Hogarth Press 1960): on page 31: p. 52; page 32: pp. 32–33; page 33: pp. 11–12, 22, and 14–15; page 34: pp. 15, 10 and 53; and page 35: pp. 53, and 19–20; the extract on page 100: p. 19. I am grateful to the estate of the author and to Chatto and Windus, as publishers, for permission.

Information about the YWCA at No. 57 was obtained from the archives of that organisation; extracts from Vere Hodgson's wartime diary were later published as *Few Eggs and No Oranges* by Dobson Books in 1976 (see pages 62–63); and Sir Basil Bartlett's *Jam Tomorrow, some early reminisces* by Elek in 1978 (see page 17).

A number of accounts of the work of Lee Abbey have been written, some of them very brief. The most valuable is *Growing in Faith*, by Richard More, one time a Chaplain at Lee Abbey in Devon. It deals with the whole Lee Abbey movement. However, since it was published in 1982 it covers only Devon and something on London. He has brought it up to date for publication in time for the Golden Jubilee under the title *The Lee Abbey Story* (1995). Inevitably he covers much the same ground as in Chapters Six and Seven here, and I warmly acknowledge any indebtedness to him. His book is strongly recommended to anyone interested in the Lee Abbey movement. The quotations from this on pages 87–88 comes from pp. 113–115, by kind favour of the author and Inter Publishing Service (IPS) Ltd.

The bi-monthly magazine of the Lee Abbey movement, *Rapport*, has some useful articles also. Jack Winslow's account on page 88 comes from his memories, reflections and hopes, entitled *The Eyelids of the Dawn* (1954), pp. 94–95 (reproduced by permission of Hodder and Stoughton Ltd). This begins with the delightful picture of growing up in the small village of Hanworth in deeply rural Middlesex, now part of the urban London sprawl. He also wrote a short book, also called *The Lee Abbey Story* (Lutterworth: 1956); the quote about the plague in Barnstaple on page 67 comes from p. 14 of that. After Winslow's death Geoffrey Rogers wrote about him in the *Lee Abbey Newsletter*, (June/July 1974) No.220, p. 3. John Murray's *A Handbook for Travellers in Devon and Cornwall* (8th Edition 1872, p. 274) provides the two quotations on pages 66–68. The scholarly work exposing 'all the legends and romances of the neighbourhood which have gathered' round the name of Wichelhalse is *A History of the Parishes of Lynton and Countisbury* by J. F. Chanter (1907). There are quotations on page 68 from this work. *Devon* by Pevsner and Cherry was a revised edition by Penguin Books in 1989 (page 69).

R. D. Blackmore's *Lorna Doone* has gone through many editions; the quotation on page 66 about Ley Manor is near the beginning of chapter XV 'Master Huckaback fails of Warrant'. The anecdote of the Anchor Cross seals given by John Donne (see pages 74–75) is told in Izaak Walton's *Life of Mr George Herbert* (bound up in A. H. Bullen's revised edition of *Walton's Lives* of 1884, pp. 277–278). Herbert's lines, and the wood-cut of the seal given to him by Donne, are on p. 278; Donne's poem to Herbert is included in Walton's *Life of Dr John Donne* on pages 59–60 of the same. Donne also gave a seal to Walton, who affixed it to his will in 1683 (*ibid* p. xli).

The Building Act of 1774 divided London houses into categories from first rate to fourth rate. These could become a little blurred. Costing over £850, ours are well into the first rate, though with about fifteen rooms they are more at the very top of the second rate. On a seven band social scale, they were occupied by those just below the very wealthy aristocracy, the really rich who were professionally among the upper civil servants both at home and overseas, the military officers, lawyers, merchants, and those with private means.

The layout of large terraced houses in general followed a long established pattern, varied only in the details. Plans of the Lee Abbey houses in Lexham Gardens are available as they exist now after many adaptations. Those given here on pages 43 and 48 are 'best guesses' after examining original floors and especially the ceiling cornices, hidden parts of which can often be discerned above false ceilings, in cupboards, etc. which have been part of alterations over many years. Conversions here for hotel uses go back to before the First World War, and other parts of our buildings have been through the process of conversion into flats at some time in their history, so that the original layout has become confused.

The plan accompanying the extract of proceedings of the Metropolitan Board of Works reproduced on page 101 is from an original with the deeds of No.100 in the possession of Noel Walker, to whom I am indebted.

This study has made no attempt to provide a careful history of the whole of the one hundred and twenty years of the existence of Lexham Gardens. However, some may be interested to know that the Iranian Embassy siege in 1980 (see page 94) was recorded by two B.B.C. men, a producer and a sound-recordist, who found themselves among the 26 men and women held hostage there. This book by Chris Cramer and Sim Harris is starkly entitled *Hostage* (1982).

In more recent years a number of people closely connected with British show business have lived in Lexham Gardens. These include Kenny Everett, Russell Harty, Derek Nimmo, Sian Phillips, Janet Reger, and Peter Witchell. Two American film stars, Tim Robbins and Susan Sarandon, lived here in the late 1980s.

For permission to use the photographs in their copyright I warmly thank Andrew Holt (*Plates 1, 2, 3a & b, 4a b & c, 14c, and 15*); the Lee Abbey Movement archives (*Plates 10, 11 a b & c* [Wallace Heaton Ltd], *12 a* [Central Photograph Co.], *12b, 13*); the Local Studies Department, Kensington and Chelsea Library, Hornton Street (*Plate 6a*); the National Monuments Record (*Plate 7* ref. 19993/4 by Bedford Lemere); The National Portrait Gallery, London (*Plate 16*); the Royal Engineers Museum, Chatham (*Plate 8a*); The rest are by the author; *Plate 8c* is from the cartoon by 'Spy' (Sir Leslie Ward) in *Vanity Fair* ('Men of the Day' DCCCLXXXIV) 28 June 1903; *Plate 8b* from *The Romantick Lady* by V. Burnett (Charles Scribner 1929); *Plate 8e* is from the Shakespeare Tercentenary Volume (East London College 1916).

Errata:

p.7 line 12: delete **a**
p.22 line 24: up **to** the age
p.30 last line of caption: **No.5 for more than eighty years**
p.51 second line from foot: Nos. 1 and **63**
p.53 nine lines up: **three** casements
p.57 seven 7 lines up: rate books. **Then** it was
p.60 lines 13-15: major internal **alterations** no doubt date
from this time.)   Presumably **these coincided**
p.81 line 21   derelict **after** the hotel days **but has since**
p.105 ten lines up: *Alumni Cantabrigienses* and *Oxonienses*
p.106 nine lines up: *Jam Tomorrow: some early **reminiscences***
p.108 line 10: for Peter Witchell read **Nicholas** Witchell.

Index